Roman Warfare

An Enthralling Guide to Ancient Rome's Army, War Strategies, and Caesar's Legacy

Free limited time bonus

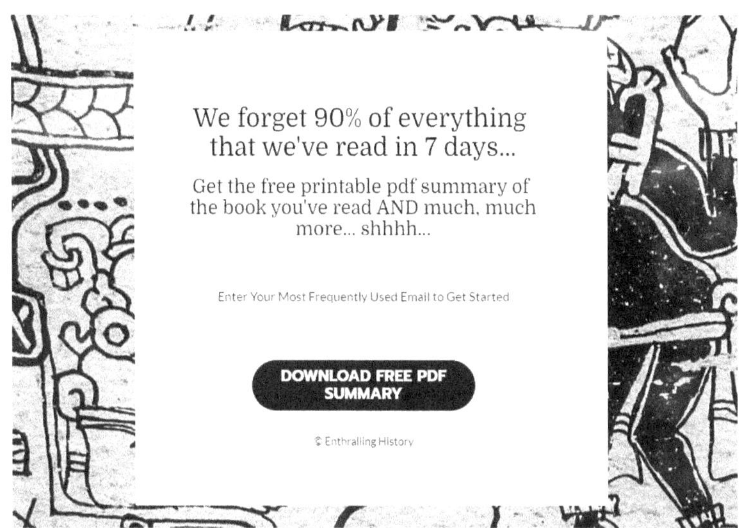

Stop for a moment. We have a free bonus set up for you. The problem is this: we forget 90% of everything that we read after 7 days. Crazy fact, right? Here's the solution: we've created a printable, 1-page pdf summary for this book that you're reading now. All you have to do to get your free pdf summary is to go to the following website: https://livetolearn.lpages.co/enthrallinghistory/

Or, Scan the QR code!

Once you do, it will be intuitive. Enjoy, and thank you!

Table of Contents

Part 1: Roman Military History

An Enthralling Guide to Battle Tactics, Empire Expansion, and the Might of the Roman Legions

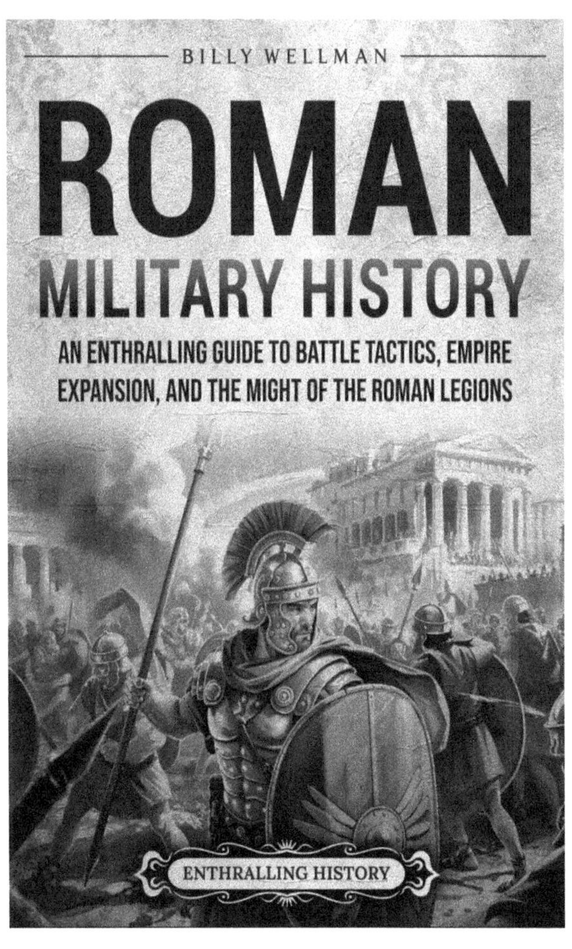

Introduction

The Roman army traces its origins to the founding of Rome in 753 BCE. The history of the Roman state is inextricably tied to the history of the Roman military; the two could not exist without one another. From humble beginnings as a citizen militia, the Roman military became a highly organized force that expanded Roman rule from Britain to North Africa and from Spain to Mesopotamia, helping shape one of the biggest empires in history.

Despite many changes in the structure of Roman leadership, the army remained a symbol of Rome's enduring strength. Throughout civil wars, foreign invasions, and even peacetime, it evolved, mirroring the society it served. Far-reaching campaigns across Europe, in Asia Minor, and across northern Africa influenced the development of siege techniques and engineering expertise, leading to the construction of sturdy, high-quality roads, many of which laid the groundwork for future transportation routes that remain in use today. Influential figures such as Gaius Marius, Sulla, Pompey, Julius Caesar, and Octavian Augustus shaped it into one of history's most formidable military machines.

The Roman army became a melting pot of cultures and one of the ways non-Romans could become citizens. The Roman state encompassed many different regions, cultures, and languages, and the army provided a way to unify these peoples. The strongest point of the Roman state was its culture, orderliness, and focus on infrastructure and organization, which existed, as if in a microcosm, in the form of the Roman military for centuries before the Roman state expanded to three continents.

Most of the biggest battles of classical antiquity were associated with the Roman army, one way or another. However, no army is immune to decline. Internal disharmony, economic pressures, corruption, and relentless invasions by Germanic tribes, the Huns, and the Persians eventually weakened and dismantled the Roman military in the West over several centuries. For more than two thousand years, the army underwent significant transformations in size, organization, equipment, and tactics. In this book, our focus will be on the development of the Roman army until the collapse of the Western Roman Empire in 476 CE. The division of the Roman Empire marked the end of an era, although the Eastern Roman Empire (the Byzantine Empire) preserved many ancient Roman military traditions for centuries to come.

This book will also show how the Roman military really functioned. In movies, TV shows, and video games, we mainly see the glorious, exciting side of the Roman military, and you will certainly experience this in the book. But we want to go further; we want to showcase the other, perhaps less exciting but equally interesting side of Roman military history. For every great day and great battle, there were countless days, months, and years of digging trenches, pitching camps, holding guard, besieging a town, and countless small skirmishes. Today, there are so many routine activities in the day-to-day life of a soldier, and it was not much different in ancient Roman times. The activities, of course, changed, but the training, long waiting, and night watches remained.

Join us on our journey through time, starting from the earliest days of the Roman military. We will voyage across centuries of military development and exciting events, stopping to catch our breath with the resting Roman armies, pitching camp for the night, and awaiting the next day's orders from generals. Our journey will end with the fall of the Western Roman Empire.

Chapter 1: The Birth of the Roman Legion

Ancient Rome's armed forces stand as one of the most effective and long-lived military institutions in recorded history. Their influence on tactics, organization, and military thinking stretched well beyond the empire's collapse. The army's main responsibilities were expansion, defending the frontier, and keeping the peace across a territory that at its height covered more than 5.9 million square kilometers (2.3 million square miles).

Rome was traditionally founded in 753 BCE. Traces of settlement in the region go back further, to the beginning of the last millennium BCE, though what exactly existed there before is difficult to say. Early Roman warfare was nothing like organized conflict. There were small raids, the occasional ritualized battle, and skirmishes that mattered more for reputation than territory. The "armies" of this period were likely small warrior bands formed around aristocratic leaders, their kin, and dependents. Glory was personal. A leader proved himself through fighting, gathered followers because of it, and built his power from the ground up.

Trying to assess the accuracy of any of this is a challenge. Romans didn't start writing their own history until the late 3rd century BCE. Everything before the Roman Republic (before 509 BCE) sits in a haze somewhere between legend and fact. Most of it is probably myth.

Romulus, Rome's first king, moved quickly to stabilize the city after its founding. There was one huge problem: there weren't enough women. A city without women would not last past a generation. Neighboring communities refused to allow marriages with Romans, closing off the usual route to alliance-building. Negotiations went nowhere.

What followed was not subtle. Early in Rome's history, Romulus is said to have organized a festival of games. This invitation was extended to neighboring peoples, including Caenina, Crustumerium, and Antemnae, along with the Sabines from Sabinum. During the festival, the Romans seized the Sabine women and drove off the men. The kings of Caenina, Crustumerium, and Antemnae invaded. Rome fought back and won each engagement.

The first to fall was Caenina and its king, Acron. Romulus marked the victory with a ceremony that Roman tradition later described as the first Roman triumph. Historians treat the whole account as legendary, with the first actual triumph belonging to the Republican period. A triumph was a ceremonial procession through the city in which the victorious commander paraded captured spoils and prisoners through Rome before making sacrifices to the gods. It would be authorized by the Senate.

After the victory, Romulus dedicated a temple to Jupiter Feretrius, the aspect of the god associated with the spoils of war. Then the Sabines themselves declared war. Battles followed. And then something unexpected happened. The Sabine women, who were now married to Romans, stopped the fighting. Livy recorded their words: "If it is kinship, if it is marriage that you cannot bear, turn your wrath against us; we are the cause of war, wounds and death of our husbands and parents. We would rather die than live without one or the other, as widows or as orphans."[i]

That was the end of the war. According to Roman tradition, the Sabines and Romans merged into a single people, ruled jointly by Titus Tatius of the Sabines and Romulus. The episode is known as either "the rape of the Sabine women" or "the abduction of the Sabine women." Historians still debate what it actually meant. Was it sexual violence? A myth constructed to explain marriage alliances and population growth? Both? The joint rule was short. Titus Tatius was said to have been killed after five years, and Romulus ruled alone again.

---

[i] Titus Livius, *From the Founding of the City*, 2012, p.45

Intervention of the Sabine Women by Jacques-Louis David (1799)[i]

Romulus is credited with founding Rome's core institutions, including the Senate and the army. His successor, Numa Pompilius, governed differently. Numa Pompilius was less interested in war. He restructured the calendar, introduced formal religious holidays, and focused on law. Livy put it plainly: "Numa wanted to rebuild the new city (already built by force and weapons) with religion and laws."[ii] Rome's third king, Tullus Hostilius, reversed that course and warred with the Sabines again.

The Roman legion likely developed from a hoplite-style phalanx, though the precise origins remain uncertain. The phalanx came from ancient Greece. A phalanx was a dense, tight block of infantry. They stood shoulder to shoulder, several ranks deep. Hoplites carried helmets, greaves, and shields. They fought as a unit. Cohesion mattered far more than individual skill; a man who broke formation endangered everyone around him. Early Roman armies seem to have fought this way.

What emerged over time was something different. The manipular legion used a checkerboard formation (the quincunx) rather than a single unbroken line. Units were spaced apart, with the gaps in one line backed

---

[i] Mesihović, Salmedin, *Orbis Romanvs,* University of Sarajevo, 2015, p.165

by units in the line behind. Three lines of infantry made up the legion. Hastati, typically the youngest soldiers, held the front. Behind them were the principes, more experienced fighters ready to push forward if the first line buckled. At the rear stood the triarii, veterans held back for the worst moments. They were committed only when things were genuinely desperate.

Each line was divided into maniples. The checkerboard pattern meant exhausted frontline soldiers could fall back through the gaps while fresh troops moved up to replace them. It also meant the formation could hold together on uneven ground, where a rigid phalanx had a tendency to fracture.

According to Livy, an early Roman legion consisted of three thousand infantry and three hundred horsemen, drawn equally from Rome's three founding tribes: the Ramnes, Tities, and Luceres.[i] Each corps of a thousand men was broken down further into ten groups of centuries, corresponding to the ten curiae of each tribe.[ii]

The three founding tribes eventually lost their importance and were replaced by a territorial system. Under reforms traditionally attributed to Servius Tullius, Rome was divided into twenty-one tribes. Four were city tribes (*tribus urbanae*)–Suburana, Esquilina, Collina, and Palatina–each named for a district of Rome. The other seventeen covered the rural countryside.

The three kings who followed Numa–Tullus Hostilius, Ancus Marcius, and Lucius Tarquinius Priscus–were remembered as warriors. Tradition credits them with campaigns against Alba Longa, the Sabines, and the Etruscan city of Veii. Tarquinius Priscus expanded the Senate by a hundred members. He also tried to reform the cavalry by creating new units outside the old tribal structure, but the augur (priest) Attus Navius blocked it. They compromised. Tarquinius Priscus would double the existing units rather than create new ones. He later celebrated victories over the Sabines and neighboring tribes.

On the cultural side, a victory over Apiolae gave the Romans occasion to establish the grounds for a circus, later the Circus Maximus. The games became one of the most enduring legacies of Roman life.

---

[i] The Ramnes were named after Romulus. Tities was named after Titus. The origins of Luceres remain unknown.

[ii] A curia is a clan-based political unit.

Two principal sources cover this period: Livy and Dionysius of Halicarnassus. Both attribute a major overhaul of Rome's political, military, and social organization to Servius Tullius, who ruled from 579 to 534 BCE. Servius doubled the number of soldiers and reorganized them by wealth. By the close of the 5th century, the army had grown to somewhere between five thousand and six thousand men, divided into centuries of up to one hundred soldiers each. Citizens were divided by age as well. Iuniores (juniors), men aged seventeen to forty-six, served in the field army, while seniores (seniors), aged forty-seven to sixty, generally handled local defense.

Each class equipped itself according to its means. The equestrians (*equites*), the wealthiest, served as cavalry. The first class of the wealthiest citizens served as heavy infantry. They had swords, long spears, and equipment resembling that of a hoplite. The second class carried similar arms but with lighter and less expensive equipment. The third and fourth classes went lighter still, armed with javelins. The fifth class, the poorest men still wealthy enough to count, likely served as skirmishers, using slings and stones.

This was the foundation of the Comitia Centuriata (Centuriate Assembly), the assembly at which the Roman people voted to declare war. Military service wasn't just a duty. It was a marker of citizenship and proof of one's standing. The five classes translated directly into centuries within the legion, binding political participation to military obligation in a way that defined what it meant to be Roman.

Anatomy of the Roman Legion

To understand the Roman army, you have to stop treating it as a single thing. It wasn't. What Servius Tullius organized in the 6th century BCE looked almost nothing like the army that fought at Cannae in 216 BCE, and neither of these armies resembles the imperial legion that held the Rhine frontier under Augustus. The Roman military evolved constantly, sometimes gradually, sometimes in response to a catastrophic defeat. Putting those three very different systems into one description produces a muddy picture.

The Servian Army (6th century BCE)

Servius reorganized Rome's military around property classes, which we covered above. The army of this period was essentially a levy of citizen infantry, organized into centuries and drawn up in a Greek-style hoplite formation. It was not even organized into cohorts; that happened much later.

The Manipular Legion (roughly 4th-2nd centuries BCE)

The real break came during the Samnite Wars, which we will cover in more detail in the next chapter. The exact timing is hard to pin down, as the shift from phalanx to manipular system was gradual rather than happening all at once. The terrain of Samnium was rugged and broken, making it poorly suited for the rigid phalanx formation that the Romans and their Latin and Etruscan contemporaries still relied on. A series of defeats, the worst of which was the humiliation at the Caudine Forks, forced the Romans to rethink their military structure.

What replaced the phalanx was more flexible. It is sometimes described as "a phalanx with joints." The key unit was no longer the phalanx but the maniple (*manipulus*). A maniple of hastati or principes typically contained around 120 men arranged in three ranks of 40 during combat. Triarii maniples were half that, about 60 men.

The first detailed account of how this worked comes from Polybius, who wrote in the mid-2nd century BCE. The manipular legion was arranged in three lines. At the front were the velites, light infantry, who engaged the enemy at the opening of a battle and worked closely with the cavalry. Behind them came the hastati, the youngest and least experienced heavy infantry, who formed the first real line of battle. The principes, more seasoned soldiers, held the second line in support. At the rear stood the triarii, the veterans, who only entered the battle when things had gone badly wrong.

According to Polybius, a standard legion comprised 10 maniples of 120 hastati, 10 maniples of 120 principes, and 10 half-strength maniples of triarii at 60 men each. Add 1,200 velites and 300 cavalry, and the total came to around 4,500 soldiers. Under serious pressure, this could be stretched to 5,000.

The Early Imperial Legion

By the early imperial period, the manipular system had given way to the cohort as the primary tactical unit. Ten cohorts made up a legion. Nine of them were standard formations of six centuries each, with a century normally containing around eighty men. The first cohort was larger and more prestigious than the others. It probably consisted of five double-strength centuries, though its exact strength is debated and likely varied.

Within each century, soldiers were grouped into *contubernia*, eight men who shared a tent or barracks room. This was the smallest unit of the army. Cavalry support in this period came mainly from auxiliary units rather than from a cavalry arm within the legion itself.

The legion's eagle standard, the aquila, was one of its most sacred symbols and was closely associated with the first cohort and its senior officers. Losing it was considered the gravest dishonor a legion could suffer. This shame could define the unit's reputation for generations.

Legion Command

The imperial legion was commanded by a legate (*legatus legionis*), usually a senator of praetorian rank. Six staff officers assisted him: a senior military tribune (*tribunus laticlavius*), also of senatorial rank and the legate's second in command, plus five equestrian tribunes (*tribuni angusticlavii*). The senior professional soldier was the camp prefect (*praefectus castrorum*). He was responsible for the fortress, its logistics, and the training of the men. In the absence of the legate, command could fall to him or to the senior tribune, depending on the situation.

Below the officers were fifty-nine centurions, each commanding a century. The five centurions of the first cohort outranked all the others. At the top of that hierarchy sat the primus pilus (literally "first spear"), who commanded the first century of the first cohort. It was the peak of an enlisted career and came with a lot of authority.

Roles Within the Century

Each century had an internal structure. The optio was the centurion's appointed deputy. He stood at the rear of the formation to keep the ranks in order. The tesserarius handled the guard roster and watch passwords. The signifer carried the centurial standard, a spear shaft hung with medallions and usually topped with an open hand, representing the oath of loyalty. In battle, soldiers kept their eyes on the standard. The signifier also managed the men's pay and savings. The cornicen, the horn blower, signaled commands.

The aquilifer carried the legion's eagle, which was different from the centurial standard. This was one of the most prestigious posts in the army. The job was given to a steady, experienced soldier who understood the tactical situation well enough to keep the eagle safe under any circumstances. The imaginifer carried an image of the emperor as a reminder of where the legion's loyalty ultimately lay. Detachments from a unit also carried their own banner, called a vexillum, that displayed their name and insignia.

Centurions were professional soldiers who had risen through the ranks. In the field, they were easy to identify. They had a transverse crest on their helmet and wore mail or scale armor and shin guards. They wore the gladius, a short stabbing sword, on the left side and the pugio, a military dagger, on the right (the reverse of an ordinary legionary), and carried a vine stick (*vitis*) as both a badge of rank and a tool for enforcing discipline. Those who had distinguished themselves might also wear phalerae, decorative medals of valor. A promotion to centurion came through demonstrated ability and appointment by senior commanders, and the pay reflected the responsibility. A centurion would be paid several times the wage of an ordinary legionary, with the exact figure depending on one's rank and the period in which they served.

The legion was largely self-sufficient. Among its men were engineers, surveyors, clerks, craftsmen, and other specialists. Many of these were classed as immunes, men excused from certain camp duties because of their skills. This arrangement kept the legion functioning as more than just a fighting force. The legion built forts wherever the threat of uprising made a permanent garrison worthwhile. The layout was standardized enough that a soldier transferred from one end of the empire to the other would recognize the plan immediately. It mirrored the layout of a Roman town with additional military buildings.

Each legion carried a number and a name. For instance, there was Legio X Gemina (the Tenth "Twin" Legion). A legion could accumulate honorifics like *pia fidelis* (dutiful and loyal) for distinguished service. Over the long history of the Roman state, legions were formed, disbanded, renumbered, and renamed. Many numbers appear more than once. What each legion kept was its own identity, history, and official titles.

Recruitment and Training

The Roman army of the imperial period was a professional force. Equipment was largely standardized and supplied. Soldiers did not generally purchase their own arms and armor, as citizen-soldiers in the early Roman Republic had done.

Recruitment drew free men from across the empire, which made for a remarkably diverse force. Soldiers posted far from home served alongside men from cultures they had never encountered. Requirements shifted over time and varied by unit, but the army's expectations were broadly consistent. One had to be physically fit, in the right age range (generally young adults), and have evidence of decent character.

According to Vegetius, who wrote in the late 4th century CE and drew heavily on earlier sources, training began not with weapons but with marching. The reasoning was that a formation is only as fast as its slowest man, and a unit that cannot march in step cannot fight in step. Recruits first had to complete 20 Roman miles (about 29.6 kilometers) in five summer hours at "military pace," carrying roughly 20.5 kilograms of kit.[i] After that came the "full pace"—24 Roman miles (about 35.5 kilometers) in the same time with the same load. Gymnastics and swimming rounded out their physical conditioning.

Weapons training followed. Vegetius says instructors were often rewarded with extra rations, which shows how seriously the army took this. Legionaries trained to thrust with the gladius while sheltering behind a large rectangular shield called a scutum. Early drills used wooden gladii and pila (a heavy javelin) against a wooden post called a quintain. The training weapons were deliberately heavier than the real thing so that the actual weapons would feel light by comparison. Later came armatura, one-on-one sparring with weapons matching the real weight; this was the same training regimen used for gladiators. Roofed halls allowed these drills to continue through winter.

Beyond individual weapons work, soldiers had to learn formation drills, such as the horn calls for attack and retreat, the role of the standards as rally points, and the different march tempos. The heavy infantry had to hold its formation under pressure, grinding forward in tight order. None of it worked unless soldiers could do it automatically, without thinking. That required repetition. The same movements were drilled over and over again until they became instinct.

Upon completion of training, the new soldier swore an oath of loyalty to the Senate and Roman people in the Republican period and to the emperor during the empire.

Service terms varied. Legionaries typically served around twenty years, with additional reserve obligations. Auxiliaries, who often served in roles that complemented the legions, including cavalry, archery, and light infantry, generally served twenty-five years. Upon honorable discharge, auxiliaries received Roman citizenship. Veterans could settle in a colony (*colonia*) with fellow soldiers or return home. Military diplomas, bronze documents recording the grant of citizenship and discharge rights, were issued to auxiliaries upon discharge.

[i] Summer hours are the longer daylight hours used in Roman timekeeping.

The Siege of Veii (406-396 BCE)

Veii was one of the most powerful cities in the Etruscan world, sitting close enough to Rome that the two had been competing for generations. As Roman power grew through the 5th century, the Romans moved to eliminate the threat permanently. Rather than risk a direct assault on Veii's strong walls, they committed to a siege that lasted nearly a decade.

Roman tradition says Marcus Furius Camillus, a Roman general and statesman of the early Roman Republic, encircled the city, cut its supply lines, and pressed the siege until Veii finally fell. Roman engineers dug tunnels and used battering rams against the walls. Eventually, they broke through the walls and the tunnels beneath them. The fall of Veii marked a major blow to Etruscan power in central Italy.

Marcus Furius Camillus by Guillaume Rouille (1553)[2]

Camillus earned the title "second founder of Rome" for his role in the victory. The campaign also marked the first time Romans paid their citizen soldiers, which was necessary in a siege that dragged on long enough to prevent men from returning to farm their land.

The Gallic Sack

The triumph over Veii was barely settled before central Italy faced a new threat. The Gauls swept south and besieged the Etruscan city of Clusium. When Rome sent envoys to negotiate, Roman tradition claimed the envoys became involved in the fighting instead of remaining neutral. The result was a disaster. The Gauls pushed deep into Roman territory, sacked much of the city, and advanced on Capitoline Hill under cover of darkness, threatening to take the last Roman stronghold.

According to Livy, what stopped them was geese. The sacred geese of Juno, kept at the temple on Capitoline Hill, heard the Gauls climbing the rocks in the night and raised the alarm. The sentinels and dogs had missed it, but the geese didn't. Marcus Manlius, a former consul, was woken by the noise, raised the men, and beat back the Gauls who had nearly reached the top. The sentinel who slept through it was executed. Manlius was honored. The Romans did not touch the geese even during the worst of the siege, when food was at its scarcest.

The ancient sources do not agree whether Camillus arrived dramatically to defeat the Gauls in battle, as the more patriotic version of the story tells it, or whether the Romans paid a ransom. The famous scene in which the Gallic leader Brennus threw his sword onto the scales and declared "Woe to the vanquished" appears in Livy, but the heroic rescue by Camillus is widely considered a later addition. What is clear is that the Gauls eventually withdrew, and Camillus, who was appointed dictator in the aftermath, oversaw the city's reconstruction. He left Rome with a second title, "second father of the city," and in some accounts, simply "Romulus."

This episode, legendary or not, left a mark on how the Romans thought about military discipline. The failure of the night watch had nearly cost them everything.

Chapter 2: Conquest of Italy: From City-State to Hegemony

Roman expansion in Italy was not a single campaign or a clean strategic vision; it was two centuries of grinding conflict, opportunistic alliances, and hard lessons that came with defeat. The process transformed Rome from a small city-state on the Tiber into the dominant power on the Italian Peninsula.

The Roman Republic itself was founded in 509 BCE, following the overthrow of King Tarquinius Superbus. The following century brought serious wars with the Etruscans. In 390 BCE, a Gallic invasion from the north nearly destroyed the city entirely. Then came the Samnites, a powerful tribal confederation from the Apennines, who would test Rome repeatedly in three separate wars. When that was finally resolved, Rome faced its last major challenge to supremacy in the Pyrrhic War in the early 3rd century BCE. Throughout it all, Rome expanded through a combination of conquest and incorporation, granting rights or full citizenship to various Italic peoples, tying them into a growing system increasingly centered on the Senate.

At the start of the Roman Republic, the dominant forces in Italy were the Etruscan cities to the north. Rome's influence among the Latin cities was limited. As Etruscan power gradually declined, it opened space for other forces, Rome among them, to assert themselves. The first known conflict between Rome and the Latin cities came at the turn of the 6th to the 5th century BCE. As Rome pushed to consolidate regional power, the Latin cities unified against the common threat, forming what became known as the Latin League. This alliance lasted for several centuries, drawing in various villages and tribes as time passed.

The war between the Romans and Latins lasted several years before ending with Rome's victory at the Battle of Lake Regillus in 496 BCE. The battle strengthened Roman influence in Latium (central western Italy), though it did not settle the question of dominance permanently; that would come later, after the Latin War of 340–338 BCE. Following the battle, a few minor skirmishes occurred before a peace treaty was established.

Dionysius of Halicarnassus records its terms: "Let there be peace between the Romans and all the Latin cities as long as the heavens and the earth shall remain where they are. Neither let them make war upon one another, nor bring in foreign enemies, nor grant safe passage to those who shall make war upon either. Let them assist one another, when warred upon, with all their forces, and let each have an equal share of the spoils and booty taken in their common wars."[i] Despite this, resentment simmered. Some Latin cities never fully accepted Rome's growing influence.

The Samnites were a formidable presence. They were a powerful tribal confederation from the Apennine highlands. They had their eyes set on the territory adjacent to Rome. The First Samnite War, traditionally dated to 343–341 BCE, began over Campania. The city of Capua and its surrounding region had appealed to Rome for protection as Samnite pressure increased, and Rome answered. The battles at Mount Gaurus and at Suessula in 343 BCE followed. Prominent Roman commanders in this early part of the war included the consul Marcus Valerius Corvinus and the war tribune Publius Decius Mus.

The Romans held their own against the Samnites, but the situation became complicated when many Latin allies began to revolt. Around 340 BCE, Rome found itself managing two threats at the same time. The battle at the Veseris River, led by consuls Publius Decius Mus and Titus Manlius Torquatus, was one of the more striking moments of the war. Publius Decius called on the pontifex maximus (the chief priest in Rome) to help him perform a ritual of *devotio*, a vow to offer his own life and those of the enemy to the gods of the underworld in exchange for victory. He then rode into the thick of battle and died. Rome won.

---

[i] Dionysius of Halicarnassus, *Roman Antiquities*, Book IV: Chapter 95, Loeb Classical Library, 1940.

There was a related ritual, *evocatio*, which worked differently. A Roman commander would call upon the enemy's own patron deity to abandon them and transfer allegiance to Rome, promising better maintenance of the cult in return. Both rituals reflect how deeply Roman commanders fused religious obligation with military command.

The disorder of the First Samnite War gave the Latin cities an opening. They sent Rome an ultimatum demanding the restoration of the previous situation between them and Rome. Rome refused. Remarkably, the Samnites, Rome's recent enemies, sided with Rome against the Latins. The Roman and Samnite forces crossed the territory of the Aequi, descended through the Apennines into Campania, and defeated the combined Latin and Campanian armies near Suessa Aurunca. The Romans then pushed through, defeating the Latins along with their Volscian and Campanian allies. By 338 BCE, the Romans had imposed their own terms.

The settlement was decisive. The cities closest to Rome were absorbed outright, and their residents were granted Roman citizenship with full rights, including *ius commercii* (the right to trade and own property) and *ius connubii* (the right to marry Romans). Only Tibur and Praeneste retained a measure of autonomy; they were treated as allies rather than subjects.

This general settlement had consequences far beyond the immediate moment. It established the framework of a confederation designed to eventually encompass all of Italy. Rome's allies supplied troops and served alongside Roman forces in shared campaigns but paid no tribute. That arrangement generated a genuine, if unequal, sense of common interest.

Before Rome could press further, it had to deal with the Samnites again. The Second Samnite War broke out in 327 BCE, sparked primarily by the contest over Neapolis (Naples). Rome's allies, the Capuans, had moved against the city, which was receiving Samnite support. Both sides found themselves drawn in through their respective obligations. The war started in Rome's favor, but the Samnite highlands were punishing terrain for Roman formations, and their momentum stalled. Neither side could break through the other's lines.

A turning point came in 325 BCE when Roman forces reached the Adriatic coast for the first time. However, a direct assault on Samnium itself brought the offensive to a halt. And in 321 BCE came a catastrophe. A Roman force of perhaps twenty thousand men was trapped at the

Caudine Forks (the Furculae Caudinae) and forced to surrender. The defeated soldiers were made to pass under a yoke of spears, wearing only their tunics. The yoke, called the *iugum*, was an ancient warrior ceremony repurposed here as deliberate humiliation; it was like a symbolic stripping of the soldiers' warrior status. Most of the men were released afterward, but supposedly six hundred hostages were left behind.

Medallion depicting the Romans going under the yoke[3]

For the Romans, this was not the end. After years of rebuilding, they went back on the offensive. The war dragged on for more than a decade as both sides fought for control of central Italy. By the early 300s BCE, Rome had regained the initiative, capturing Bovianum, a key Samnite city, around 305 BCE and pressing on to take places such as Fregellae, Calatia, and Nola. The struggle finally ended with a peace treaty in 304 BCE. The agreement did not destroy Samnite independence, but it forced them to recognize the growing power of Rome.

The peace did not hold. In 299 BCE, the Gauls and Etruscans invaded Roman territory. A potential Samnite alliance with these forces threatened to undo everything Rome had built. The Third Samnite War began in 298 BCE. Rome responded by advancing into Etruscan territory while those forces were occupied elsewhere, effectively neutralizing them.

The decisive engagement came at Sentinum in 295 BCE. Rome committed four legions. One of the consuls, Publius Decius Mus, performed a devotio before the battle; this was the same ritual his father had performed at Veseris half a century earlier. Rome won. The Etruscans negotiated peace, and the Samnites were crushed.

What remained of Samnite territory was absorbed or reorganized. Most came under Roman control, and the rest of the lands were incorporated as *civitas sine suffragio*, cities without voting rights. They were subject to Rome's authority without representation in its assemblies. Central Italy was now Roman. In 283 BCE, Rome repelled a Gallic incursion at Lake Vadimo, effectively closing the chapter on major internal Italian resistance.

Two figures from the Third Samnite War are worth talking about. Manius Curius Dentatus, the general who ultimately broke Samnite resistance, was a *homo novus*, a man without aristocratic lineage who had risen through ability and popular support rather than family connections. Later Roman accounts speak of how he embodied Republican virtues. He took only a modest plot of land, farmed it himself, and refused personal enrichment. His biography became a template for generations. The other notable commander was Lucius Cornelius Scipio Barbatus, whose tombstone Livy mentions as the earliest Roman inscription naming a historical figure.

After the Samnites, Rome's expansion brought it into contact with the Greek colonies of southern Italy. The most powerful was Tarentum, a Spartan colony and a major Mediterranean city. Tensions with Rome dated to 282 BCE, when a Roman fleet entered waters near Tarentum in violation of an earlier treaty. The citizens of Tarentum attacked the Roman ships and insulted the envoys Rome sent in response. Rome dispatched a consul to negotiate. The Tarentines responded by calling in outside help. This help was none other than Pyrrhus, King of Epirus.

Pyrrhus was an ambitious man in a complicated position. He had designs on the Macedonian throne but no firm grip on it. The invitation from Tarentum offered him a chance to strengthen his standing. In 280 BCE, he arrived in Italy with around twenty-two thousand soldiers, three thousand cavalry, and approximately twenty war elephants. The Romans sent a force under Consul Valerius Levinus. The armies met near Heraclea, on the Siris River in 280 BCE. Rome lost. Several tribes, including the Samnites, shifted allegiance to Pyrrhus.

Pyrrhus of Epirus[4]

The second battle came at Asculum in Apulia in 279 BCE. Two brutal days of fighting left the Romans with around six thousand dead. Pyrrhus lost roughly half that. He had technically won, but the cost rattled him. He reportedly responded, "Another such victory and we are lost." That is where the phrase "Pyrrhic victory" comes from. It was not the tactical outcome alone, but more so Pyrrhus's own recognition that winning at this rate was indistinguishable from losing. His army was smaller to begin with. He could not replace men the way Rome could. He sent terms saying Rome should dissolve its Italian alliances and leave the Greek cities of the south alone. Rome declined.

Around this time, the Galatians had invaded Macedonia and Greece, another crisis that complicated Pyrrhus's long-term ambitions since he still coveted the Macedonian throne. Carthage, watching Pyrrhus's campaigns with concern about its own interests in Sicily, made a pact with Rome. Neither side would negotiate a separate peace with the Greeks.

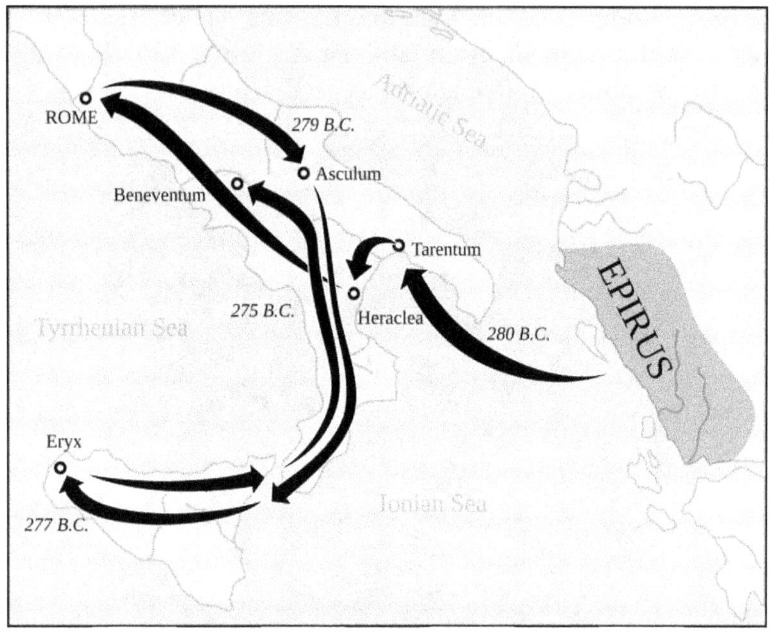

Battle sites of the Pyrrhic War[5]

One episode from this period has stuck in historical memory, repeated for centuries as an example of Roman character. A consul named Gaius Fabricius was sent to negotiate prisoner exchanges with Pyrrhus. The king, having heard of Fabricius's reputation for integrity, tried to buy him. He offered lavish gifts, which Fabricius rejected. At a later meeting, Pyrrhus arranged for an elephant to rear up behind Fabricius during negotiations, apparently hoping to unsettle him. Fabricius didn't even flinch. "Just as I was not swayed by your wealth yesterday," he said, "I am even less afraid of your elephant today."[i] Pyrrhus's own physician then approached Fabricius privately and offered to poison the king for a fee. Fabricius reported the offer to Pyrrhus, who had the physician executed. He then released all Roman prisoners without conditions. Rome released its own captives in return. However, peace failed because neither Rome nor Pyrrhus was willing to compromise.

---

[i] Mesihović, Salmedin, *Orbis Romanvs*, University of Sarajevo, 2015, p.272-273

In 278 BCE, Pyrrhus shifted his focus to Sicily, capturing several cities including Palermo, Seleste, and Selinunte. He failed at Lilybaeum, which stopped his momentum and began to erode his support among the Sicilian Greeks. While he was occupied in Sicily, Rome was racking up victories over the Samnites and other Italian tribes in 278, 277, and 276 BCE. Pyrrhus finally made the tough decision to return to Italy.

The decisive engagement came at Beneventum in 275 BCE. Roman archers scattered the Greek war elephants, which turned on their own lines. Rome won. The city's name was changed from Maleventum, meaning something like "ill wind," to Beneventum, meaning "good event."[i] Manius Curius Dentatus celebrated a triumph in Rome with four captured elephants parading through the city.

Pyrrhus left Italy in 275 BCE, leaving Tarentum under the command of a garrison. The city held its fortifications until 272 BCE, when it was forced to surrender. It gave hostages to Rome and dismantled its fleet. Among those taken to Rome in the aftermath was a Tarentine Greek named Livius Andronicus, though whether he came as a hostage or in some other capacity is debated. He went on to become one of the earliest Latin authors. Pyrrhus himself died in 272 BCE at Argos. He was killed during street fighting against the forces of Antigonus II Gonatas.

With Pyrrhus gone and Tarentum neutralized, the Samnites accepted Roman supremacy at last. Under Roman command, they helped take the Etruscan city of Volsinii in 264 BCE. That is generally regarded as the end of the conquest of Italy.

The whole process took roughly two centuries, though the military effort was far from continuous. Most of Rome's opponents were tribal forces without unified political structures or the resources to sustain prolonged campaigns. As Rome itself changed, growing from a cluster of villages into a city with a large population and an organized state, its approach to war changed with it. What began as ritualized raids and skirmishes between aristocrats became a machine. Rome had a state-funded, state-organized professional army capable of sustained campaigns across an entire peninsula. The next stage would take that machine beyond Italy entirely, toward Sicily, Corsica, Sardinia, and the coast of North Africa.

---

[i] Mirković, Miroslava, *Istorija Rimske države*, Službeni glasnik, 2014, p.104

Chapter 3: The Punic Wars: Clashes with Carthage

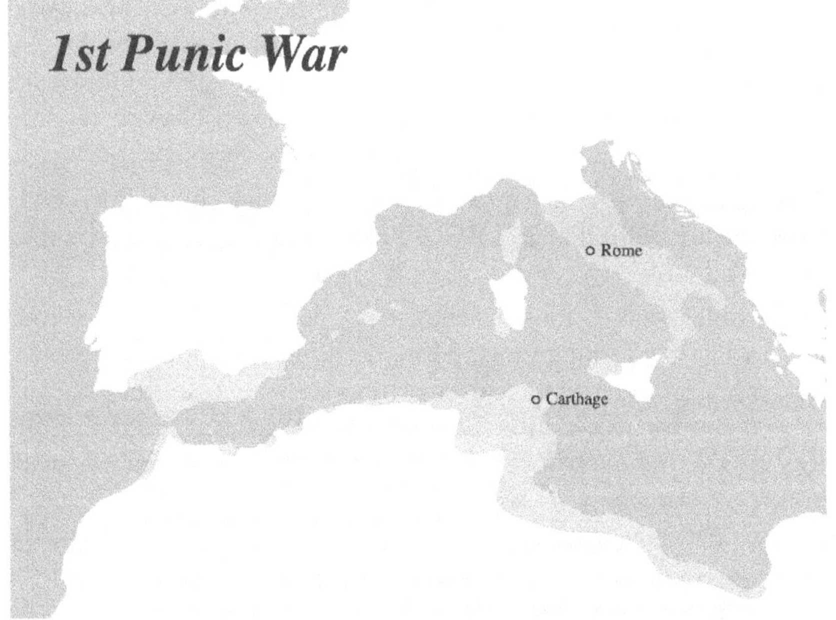

Lands owned by Romans and Carthaginians before the First Punic War[6]

After two centuries of grinding warfare, Rome had forged an Italian confederacy and emerged as one of the most formidable powers in the Mediterranean world. Its military strength in terms of manpower, organization, and strategic depth gave it exceptional capabilities that few rivals could match.

After defeating Pyrrhus, a skilled commander who had tested Rome, the Roman Republic became a power that others wanted on their side. Egypt was the first major Hellenistic kingdom to open diplomatic relations in 273 BCE. Various Greek city-states took note of Rome's rise as well. And Carthage, the great Phoenician colonial power with deep commercial and political stakes across the western Mediterranean, watched closely because Roman foreign policy was beginning to affect Carthaginian interests.

The treaty between Rome and Carthage, first established in the 6th century, was revised in 279 BCE during the war against Pyrrhus. Once the southern Italian ports came under Roman control, the interests of Naples and Tarentum folded into Rome's orbit as well. A collision between the two powers was becoming increasingly likely. There is a tradition that says Pyrrhus, on leaving Italy, remarked that he was "leaving the battleground for Romans and Carthaginians."[1] Whether he said it or not, the observation came true.

On land, Rome was clearly the stronger force. At sea, Carthage had no serious rival. Each was backed by substantial allies. Rome was backed by the Etruscans, Samnites, Umbrians, and Italian Greeks (most of them were Roman allies or subjects by this point). Carthage was supported by the Berber and Libyan peoples from its North African territories. The collision, when it came, began in Sicily.

The trigger was the Mamertines, Campanian mercenaries who had seized the city of Messana around 288 BCE and established themselves there by force. Hiero II, ruler of Syracuse and the only significant independent power left on the island, raised an army to deal with them. The Mamertines were divided. Some wanted to appeal to Rome. Others preferred Carthage, which had the fleet to reach them quickly and already maintained ports in Sardinia, Corsica, and southern Iberia. Rome understood what was at stake. Carthaginian control of Messana would put a major hostile naval power just across the water from the Italian coast.

The Roman Senate could not agree on what to do, so the decision was pushed to the citizen assembly, the Comitia Centuriata, which was persuaded by the prospect of plunder and new territory. Appius Claudius Caudex was appointed consul and sent with a force to Messana. The Mamertines requested that he take control of the city. Carthage,

---

[1] Mirković, Miroslava, *Istorija Rimske države*, Službeni glasnik, 2014, p.123

meanwhile, allied with Hiero to defend Syracuse. That friction ignited the First Punic War in 264 BCE.

Two years in, after negotiations went nowhere, the Romans laid siege to Agrigentum, the Greek colony known as Akragas, one of Carthage's key strongholds on the island. The siege dragged on for six months. Carthage sent a relief force under Hanno, reportedly comprising fifty thousand infantry, six thousand cavalry, and sixty war elephants. The Romans, fielding a force that ancient sources put at a substantial size, drove Hanno back and eventually took the city. It was a serious blow.

Losing Agrigentum pushed Carthage toward its natural advantage: the sea. While Carthage pressed Rome's coastal positions with its fleet, the Romans scrambled to build one of their own. Until this point, their naval forces had consisted mainly of ships contributed by allies like Tarentum, Elea, and Neapolis (the *socii navales*). Rome had no real tradition of naval warfare. What it built was a solution to that problem.

Unfamiliar with open-water tactics, the Romans leaned into what they knew: close combat. Their ships were fitted with a boarding device called the corvus, a spiked gangplank that could be dropped onto an enemy deck, locking the ships together and turning a sea battle into something resembling a land engagement. The first test, at the Lipari Islands, went badly. But at Mylae in 260 BCE, under Consul Gaius Duilius, Rome won its first real naval victory. Duilius celebrated with a triumph in Rome and was honored with a columna rostrata, a column decorated with the prows of captured enemy ships.

Roman corvus naval boarding device[7]

Emboldened, Rome went further. A fleet of 330 ships was assembled and sent toward Africa. The commanders were Consuls Marcus Atilius Regulus and Lucius Manlius Vulso. The Carthaginian fleet was commanded by Hanno and Hamilcar. The battle that followed, at Cape Ecnomus in 256 BCE, was one of the largest naval engagements in ancient history. Carthage brought around 350 ships. The Romans had 330, plus the corvus. The boarding device proved decisive, and Rome won. The expeditionary force, around 140,000 men in total, landed on African soil not long after.

Local Numidian tribes, themselves in conflict with Carthage, joined in attacking the city. Carthage was forced to open peace negotiations. Regulus demanded, among other things, the surrender of the Carthaginian fleet and the payment of a massive tribute. These terms were so harsh that Carthage had no real choice but to fight on. They brought in a Spartan mercenary commander, Xanthippus of Lacedaemon, who reorganized the Carthaginian army and used their elephants and cavalry to devastating effect in open terrain. The Romans were routed, and Regulus was captured.

A new Roman fleet was sent to evacuate the survivors. It succeeded, but on the return voyage, the fleet was caught in a catastrophic storm off Sicily and almost entirely destroyed. The disaster wiped out most of the men and ships Rome had committed to the African campaign.

Despite that catastrophe, the war ground on for another fifteen years. Rome won battles across Sicily, cutting Carthaginian supply lines and steadily tightening control. It ended in 241 BCE at the Battle of the Aegates Islands, where Rome destroyed the Carthaginian fleet and forced a peace settlement. Sicily became Rome's first overseas territory.

The victory came at a steep price. Rome had lost enormous numbers of men and multiple fleets, many of them to storms. Coastal regions had been raided and devastated. However, Carthage had suffered worse. Its military was largely mercenary, and paying those men after a string of defeats strained its finances to the breaking point. Rebellions broke out in Libya and Sardinia. Hamilcar Barca (not the same Hamilcar at the Battle of Cape Ecnomus) and Hanno eventually suppressed them, but the effort depleted what little of Carthaginian resilience remained. Rome had won, but just barely. It had been expensive, and the Romans had no illusions about how close it had been.

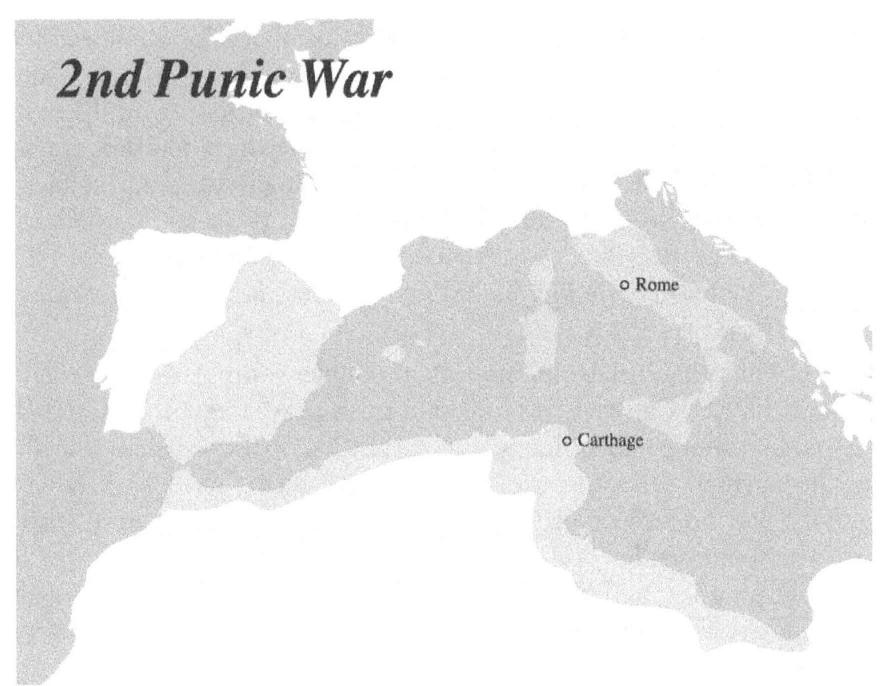

Lands owned by the Romans and Carthaginians before the Second Punic War[8]

Shortly after suppressing the mercenary rebellions, Hamilcar shifted his focus to Spain. The Iberian Peninsula was rich in silver, manpower, and land, and Hamilcar used all of it to rebuild Carthaginian strength from the ground up. He died in 228 BCE, and his son-in-law, Hasdrubal, took over. Hasdrubal's command was cut short, as he was assassinated in 221 BCE. Hamilcar's twenty-six-year-old son Hannibal was chosen to replace him.

The Second Punic War did not begin simply with Hannibal's rise to command. It was triggered in 219 BCE when Hannibal besieged Saguntum, a city that Rome considered under its protection. Rome demanded that Carthage surrender Hannibal, but Carthage refused. The war began formally in 218 BCE. What followed was one of the most daring campaigns in ancient history, not because Hannibal fought Rome on Roman terms but because he refused to.

The Romans' plan was to bring the war to Carthage so the fighting would be far from Italy. Hannibal anticipated this and moved first. He crossed the Pyrenees, pushed through southern Gaul, and then did something that still defies easy explanation: he crossed the Alps in late autumn of 218 BCE with tens of thousands of soldiers, cavalry, and war elephants. His army had been assembled largely in Spain, though it also included Libyan heavy troops and Numidian cavalry. These men were suited to open terrain and warm climates, not mountain passes in late October.

The losses during the crossing were severe. That he came through at all was extraordinary. Since this is primarily a book about Roman military history, we won't dwell on the mechanics of the crossing itself, but it tells us something important about Rome. The Romans expected enemies to behave as they did, to settle into winter camps, rest, and wait for spring. Campaigning slowed in winter, but it rarely stopped entirely. Hannibal's appearance in northern Italy in autumn, when the Romans expected the usual lull, caused panic.

Hannibal spent the march building alliances where he could, particularly with Gallic tribes who had their own grievances against Rome. These alliances were never guaranteed. Some tribes resisted him outright, while many others held back and waited to see how the early battles went before committing to either side. Hannibal understood that he was operating in entirely unfamiliar territory, deep in enemy country, far from any Carthaginian base. Friendly locals meant food, intelligence, and security for his flanks. He needed all three. For much of the march, he pushed forward largely on his own, battling the resistance of natives along the route as much as the terrain itself. The conditions were punishing, and the army that descended from the Alps into northern Italy was a fraction of what had set out.

The first significant clash came at the Ticino River in 218 BCE. The Roman consul Publius Cornelius Scipio had been heading for Spain when the scale of Hannibal's advance forced him to turn back. What happened at the Ticino was not a full pitched battle; it was primarily a cavalry engagement, with both sides probing rather than committing everything they had. Ancient battles often worked this way. The two armies would shadow each other for days, generals drawing their men into formation and then standing them down again, watching the enemy's movements and waiting for ground and weather that suited them. Soldiers in those camps knew the enemy was sometimes only a few kilometers away. They were close enough to hear them and, in some cases, could see their movements. They had to live with that knowledge while the waiting dragged on.

When the engagement at the Ticino River finally came, Hannibal's cavalry proved decisive. Roman velites (light infantry) advanced and prepared to throw their javelins. The Carthaginian horsemen charged before they could release them. The velites pulled back in a hurry. Roman and Gallic cavalry moved up to counter but found their advance tangled with the retreating skirmishers; they couldn't build any momentum. Then a part of the Carthaginian cavalry swung wide and threatened not only the oncoming Roman horsemen but the small escort surrounding Scipio himself. That was the moment that broke the battle. The velites fled, and the Roman line unraveled. Scipio was badly wounded. Tradition holds he was pulled from the field by his teenage son, who bore the same name, Publius Cornelius Scipio. The Romans retreated across the river.

They fell back to Piacenza. There, Gallic allies who had been fighting alongside Rome began to waver, then broke entirely. Around two thousand of them joined Hannibal in an act of open mutiny. They had watched Scipio lose and chose who they thought would be the ultimate victor. At the Ticino River, Hannibal had committed perhaps six thousand of his roughly twenty-six thousand men. He had won with a fraction of his force, and now, he had Gallic troops joining him.

The defeat alarmed Rome enough that the Senate sent the second consul, Tiberius Sempronius Longus, north to reinforce Scipio. The Battle of the Trebia, sometime in late December 218 BCE, would be on an entirely different scale from the skirmish at the Ticino River.

The two armies took up positions on opposite banks of the Trebia. They spent days watching each other. Before the main battle, a skirmish broke out. A Carthaginian raiding party sent to plunder nearby settlements was intercepted by Roman forces and took heavy casualties. The Romans were elated. They had bloodied Hannibal's men and forced him to pull back. Longus took this as a sign that the moment had come to end the invasion with one decisive blow. It was his biggest mistake.

Hannibal had set a trap and was simply waiting for the Romans to walk into it. He had already positioned his younger brother Mago with a force of around two thousand mixed cavalry and infantry, concealed in the scrub near the riverbank, well away from the Carthaginian camp. He had ordered his own men to be fed and warmed before dawn, ensuring they were ready for battle. Early in the morning, his Numidian cavalry crossed the Trebia and began harassing the Roman camp. The Numidians were pushed back, but then they came straight back and harassed the Romans again. Longus, commanding roughly forty thousand men, including Roman legions and allied contingents, took the bait. He ordered his army across the river without waiting for breakfast and without time for the river to warm up.

Crossing the Trebia in December was brutal. On horseback, it was difficult enough. For the infantry, it was something else. The water was chest-deep in places and freezing. The men arrived on the far bank cold, wet, and hungry before a battle that was already underway. The Roman heavy infantry pushed hard in the center nonetheless, as it always did, and for a time, the Romans seemed to be getting the better of Hannibal's center. However, on the flanks, it was a different story. Carthaginian cavalry overpowered the Roman horsemen on both sides and drove them from the field, then wheeled back to hit the Roman rear. Mago's concealed force came out of hiding and struck from behind.

The Roman center was being ground down from three directions at once. The light infantry and cavalry were gone. Longus, seeing that the bulk of his force had been broken, ordered a retreat. A core of around ten thousand men, those in the tightest formation, managed to cut through the Carthaginian center and make it back to Piacenza. Most of the other men were killed or captured.

Longus returned to Rome to oversee elections for the following year's consuls. The new consuls for 217 BCE were Gaius Flaminius and Gnaeus Servilius Geminus.

Before reaching the battlefield, Hannibal had to cross the Arno marshes. The army waded through floodwater for four days and three nights. The water was up to their chests in places, and soldiers rested on the bodies of dead horses when they could find nowhere dry to stand. The losses were severe. They lost horses, men, and almost all of the remaining elephants. Only one elephant survived. Hannibal himself contracted a severe eye infection during the crossing that eventually cost him the sight in one eye. He recovered and kept moving.

Flaminius stationed his forces near Arretium to block Hannibal's route south. Hannibal bypassed him. This was a deliberate slight designed to draw Flaminius out in a hurry without giving him time to think. It worked. Flaminius commanded four legions and was burning to confront Hannibal directly. The Gallic tribes of the north were increasingly drifting toward Carthage, unsure whether Rome could stop the invasion, and Flaminius knew that every day without a fight cost Rome allies. He marched fast.

The ground near Lake Trasimene was made for an ambush. Hills rose on one side, the lake cut off any retreat on the other, and a long, narrow passage ran between them. During the night before the battle, Hannibal sent cavalry, light infantry, and heavy infantry on a night march to take positions in the hills along the lakeshore. The main camp stayed visible. The Romans were meant to see it and follow it in.

On June 21st, 217 BCE, Flaminius led his army into the passage. The Romans marched in column, as was standard—three parallel lines suited for movement, to be reformed into battle order once they reached the enemy. They never got that far.

When Hannibal judged that enough Romans had entered the trap, he gave the signal. The attack came simultaneously from the front, from the hills above, and from behind. The Romans were struck before they could form up, with the lake blocking any retreat to the right. It was chaos. Flaminius was killed in the fighting. Later tradition attributed his death to a Gallic nobleman named Ducarius. Roman casualties numbered around fifteen thousand killed. Several thousand more were captured in the days that followed. A portion of the army managed to escape the trap, though for most, there was no way out. Geminus, marching separately and completely unaware that the battle was even happening, sent his cavalry ahead to link up with Flaminius. They rode directly into Hannibal's forces and were wiped out. Geminus pulled his four legions back to Ariminum.

What Hannibal demonstrated in these three engagements was a consistent and ruthless pattern: provoke, lure, fix, then hit from every direction at once. At Trebia, he had goaded a larger army into a freezing river before dawn and then collapsed its flanks. At Trasimene, he had lured an entire army into a pocket with no exit and attacked before it could even form up. The Romans were not stupid or cowardly. They simply expected enemies to fight as they did, in open formation on chosen ground. Hannibal's methods were unlike anything Roman commanders had been trained to anticipate or counter.

Trasimene scared the Senate badly enough to do something it rarely did when the Roman Republic was functioning as intended. The senators wanted to appoint a dictator. Quintus Fabius Maximus was given supreme command. He was neither the first nor the last Roman to hold the office. Later, men like Sulla, Gaius Marius, Pompey, and Caesar would eventually push the institution far beyond its original purpose. Fabius was not that kind of man, though. He took the emergency powers because the situation required them, used them as the laws intended, and did not try to hold onto them longer than necessary. He was simply tasked with dealing with the Carthaginian threat.[i]

[i] The office of dictator, in its original form, did not have absolute power. He did have more power

His strategy was simple, deeply unpopular, and almost certainly right. He refused to meet Hannibal in open battle. Instead, Fabius shadowed the Carthaginian army across Italy, attacking supply parties, harassing foragers, cutting access to food wherever he could, and declining battle every time Hannibal offered it. The Romans gave him a nickname for it. He became known as Cunctator (the "Delayer"), and they did not mean it kindly, at least not at first. However, Fabius had understood something that Flaminius and Longus had not. Hannibal could not replace his losses. Every skirmish that killed Carthaginians was men that Hannibal could never get back. Rome, with its deep reserves of manpower and its ability to levy new legions after even catastrophic defeats, could absorb punishment that would cripple another army. The math favored patience.

The daily reality of the campaign under Fabius was grinding and unglamorous. The army was in almost constant motion. Camps were thrown up in the evening and dismantled the next morning so the army could move again. Soldiers were placed into formation, marched toward the enemy, and then marched back without a battle having taken place, sometimes for days on end. The enemy camp was occasionally visible, sometimes close enough that the two sides could hear each other. But the order would always come to stand down. For ordinary soldiers, that kind of sustained tension without resolution was its own form of punishment.

Night watches (the *vigiliae*) were strictly enforced. The night was divided into four watches between sunset and sunrise, and soldiers rotated through them so that no one man bore the full burden. Abandoning a watch or being caught asleep at post was not a minor infraction. Offenders could be beaten to death by their own comrades, a punishment called *fustuarium*. It was carried out after a formal court martial and on the authority of appropriate officers, like consuls, praetors, or legionary commanders.

The watches guarded against night attacks, as well as fire, theft, and the general disorder that could unravel a large force camping in the open. Keeping proper watches required reliable timekeeping. Timekeeping in the field could be managed using clepsydrae, water clocks, though in practice, the camps relied more on signals and scheduled guard rotations than on precise measurement. The principle of the clepsydra was simple enough. Water poured into a vessel with a small hole at the bottom, and

---

than the consuls, who were directly subordinate to him. Dictators could still be held accountable by the Senate and could only exert authority in areas for which they were appointed. They defended the state and organized public games, religious rituals, and many other activities.

the passage of time was marked by how much had drained. More sophisticated versions with mechanical elements existed and were used by civilians, but armies tended toward the more practical version.

Hannibal plundered as he moved, trying to feed his army off enemy territory and demonstrating to Rome's Italian allies that Rome could not protect them. Fabius countered with scorched-earth measures where he could, denying Hannibal food. Reportedly, he also ordered significant increases in sacrifices during this period. Crops and livestock were said to be burned in large quantities to appease the gods. Whatever the religious rationale, it reduced what Hannibal's foragers could find.

It was not a sustainable situation for Rome, as the public was impatient. Months passed. Hannibal ranged across Italy, and Fabius followed him. Nothing seemed to change in the Romans' eyes. A cavalry commander named Marcus Minucius demonstrated during a brief period when Fabius was away (he was likely in Rome for religious ceremonies) that he could at least make the Carthaginians feel pressure, challenging them on the battlefield rather than merely hovering nearby. A plebeian tribune named Metilius, who understood how to work public sentiment, pushed for Minucius to be elevated. The result was something almost without precedent. Minucius was granted powers equal to those of the dictator, effectively splitting command of the Roman army in two. Whether he was formally a co-dictator is uncertain, but in practice, he commanded half the legions.

Near Geronium in early autumn 217 BCE, with both commanders and their respective forces present, Hannibal saw his opening. He sent some of his best troops out under the cover of night to conceal themselves in hollows in the broken terrain below the Carthaginian camp, hidden from view. Then he drew his main force out in the open, inviting a response from the Roman army. Minucius took the bait. He sent his light infantry forward. They clashed with Hannibal's troops and reached a stalemate. He committed his cavalry to break the deadlock, but the cavalry began to take losses. So, he called up the heavy infantry.

The Romans were pressing up the hill when the hidden troops came out of concealment and hit them from behind and both flanks simultaneously. The Roman force came apart. They retreated in disorder. Fabius marched his legions out, and Hannibal, unwilling to face the combined Roman force, withdrew to his camp. Minucius was not formally stripped of his command, but his authority quietly folded back under Fabius's from that point forward.

Near the Aufidus River, close to the town of Cannae in Apulia, came the worst single day in Roman military history. The Battle of Cannae in 216 BCE was not merely a defeat. It was an annihilation. Tribunes, senators, and tens of thousands of soldiers died in a single afternoon. The exact figures from ancient sources vary and are likely exaggerated, but the scale of the disaster was real enough. Hannibal's double envelopment—drawing the massive Roman center forward while his flanks curved around and closed behind it—became the most studied tactical maneuver in military history. Commanders were still trying to replicate it two thousand years later.

Rome lowered the recruitment age to about seventeen and levied additional legions. In an act of genuine desperation, the Senate authorized two legions formed from slaves purchased by the state. They had been freed and armed for service, something essentially without precedent in Roman history. This allowed Rome to keep fighting. This was perhaps the most remarkable thing about Rome in the Second Punic War, and Hannibal likely understood it better than anyone. Every time he destroyed a Roman army, Rome raised another one. The Roman Republic's capacity to absorb catastrophic losses and reconstitute itself made it almost impossible to defeat in the way a conventional war could be won. Strategically, Hannibal outmaneuvered every Roman commander he faced. However, strategy alone could not end a war against an enemy that simply refused to accept defeat.

Marcus Claudius Marcellus was sent to Sicily and eventually laid siege to Syracuse. Hiero II's death and the subsequent shift of Syracuse toward Carthage led to Marcellus camping outside the city's walls. The siege lasted from around 214 to 212 BCE. It was prolonged considerably by one man: Archimedes. The mathematician, physicist, and engineer designed and built defensive systems that repeatedly stopped Roman assaults. Cranes reached over the walls to lift ships and capsize them, and artillery rained stones on approaching soldiers. These were mechanisms the Romans had never encountered and struggled to counter. Eventually, the Romans found a way in. The city fell and was thoroughly plundered. Marcellus had wanted Archimedes taken alive, as he recognized what the man was worth. One account records a Roman soldier finding Archimedes working on a math problem during the sack of the city. He ordered Archimedes to come before Marcellus. Archimedes refused, as he needed to finish what he was doing. The soldier killed him. Marcellus was furious.

While the Italian war ground on, Rome was systematically dismantling Carthaginian power in Spain. Publius Cornelius Scipio, the consul's son who had reportedly pulled his wounded father from the field at the Ticino River years before, was sent to Spain in 210 BCE. The Senate granted him imperium through a special decree, making him the first person to receive such authority without holding a magistracy.[i] In 209 BCE, he captured Cartagena (New Carthage), the primary Carthaginian base in Spain. By 206 BCE, with local tribal support, he had cleared Carthaginian forces from the entire southern Iberian Peninsula.

Back in Italy, the balance was shifting. When Capua appealed to Hannibal for help against Rome in 211 BCE, he marched his army to the very walls of Rome in a show of force that gave rise to the phrase "Hannibal ante portas" ("Hannibal is at the gates"). Rome panicked.

However, Hannibal did not assault the city. He lacked the siege equipment. He turned back south, and Capua fell to Rome. The decision not to attack, whether forced on him by circumstance or a genuine strategic choice, diminished his standing in Carthage.

Something worse happened in 207 BCE. His brother Hasdrubal Barca had crossed the Alps with a relief force, hoping to link up with Hannibal in Italy. He never made it. Hasdrubal was intercepted and killed at the Battle of the Metaurus before he could reach his brother. Rome sent Hasdrubal's severed head south to Hannibal's camp. Whatever realistic hope Hannibal had held of receiving reinforcement from Carthage largely died with his brother.

Scipio was elected consul in 205 BCE. In 204 BCE, he crossed to Africa with an invasion force. Two years later, in 202 BCE, the two greatest commanders of the war faced each other at Zama. Hannibal had been recalled from Italy to defend Carthage itself. That battle ended the war. Rome had won, although it came at enormous cost and took a very long time.

At Zama in 202 BCE, Hannibal made his stand. He had slightly more infantry and around eighty elephants, but the Romans held the decisive advantage in cavalry. The Numidian king, Masinissa, had switched sides and brought his experienced horsemen with him. It cost Hannibal the battle. Carthaginian casualties were far heavier, around 20,000 killed, while Roman losses were much smaller, roughly 1,500. It was Hannibal's

[i] Imperium was the legal authority granted by the Roman state to command armies.

first decisive defeat as overall commander; he had faced setbacks before, but nothing like this. Fifteen years of campaigning in Italy, army after army destroyed, and in the end, it came down to a cavalry engagement he just could not win.

A marble bust thought to be of Hannibal[9]

Peace was concluded in 201 BCE. The terms were punishing. Carthage could keep its African territory but had to surrender everything overseas. Most of the fleet was gone. Heavy reparations were imposed. Politically, Hannibal survived the defeat better than might be expected. He went on to serve as a political leader, a suffete, in Carthage and reportedly pushed through reforms that made him enemies among the Punic aristocracy. Roman pressure eventually forced him into exile around 195 BCE. He made his way first to the court of Antiochus III of the Seleucid Empire, where he offered his services against Rome. Later accounts place him in Armenia and Crete before he eventually settled in Bithynia, near Anatolia. The Romans tracked him there too, threatening the Bithynian king to hand him over. Hannibal had no intention of being taken alive. Most ancient sources agree he committed suicide by poison rather than falling into Roman hands. The exact year is debated—somewhere between 183 and 181 BCE—but the manner of his death is consistent across the main traditions.

The fifty years between the Second and Third Punic Wars were not peaceful for Carthage. The city recovered economically, regaining considerable wealth through agriculture and trade, which only deepened Roman suspicion. Meanwhile, the Numidians flourished under Masinissa, and Rome consistently backed him in his repeated territorial clashes with Carthage. These conflicts were the main problem. When Carthage finally took up arms against the Numidians without Rome's permission, it violated the terms of its treaty, which gave Rome the opening it wanted.

By this point, Rome had accumulated enough military and political strength to act on multiple fronts simultaneously. It had already dealt with Macedonia in the eastern Mediterranean. When the Third Punic War came, it was less a war than an execution.

The man who pushed hardest for it was Marcus Porcius Cato, better known as Cato the Elder. He knew Carthage's wealth firsthand and was not shy about his opinions. His speeches in the Senate became famous. No matter what the subject, he ended them the same way: "Ceterum censeo Carthaginem delendam esse" ("Furthermore, I think that Carthage must be destroyed"). He said it so often that it became a joke, but it eventually turned into reality.

Before formally declaring war, Rome imposed increasingly harsh demands on Carthage, pushing its adversary toward submission. A confrontation between Carthage and the Numidians gave Rome its formal pretext, and war was declared. The Romans initially hoped to take the city quickly by force. They were wrong about that. Carthage's walls were formidable, and its defenders were desperate. The siege dragged on for years. It continued until 147 BCE, when Publius Cornelius Scipio Aemilianus arrived in Africa and took command. He moved to cut off supply routes, defeated the Carthaginian field armies operating outside the city, and tightened the stranglehold. Near the end of the siege, Hasdrubal the Boetharch, the commander of the Carthaginian forces, surrendered to Scipio directly.

The assault on the city itself began in 146 BCE. There were six days of brutal street fighting. On the seventh day, the Romans seized the Byrsa, the citadel of Carthage. Hasdrubal had taken refuge with his family in a temple, apparently intending to die there. When the Romans arrived, he instead went to Scipio and asked for mercy. His wife, watching from above, did not spare him her contempt. She condemned him publicly for saving himself, then threw herself and their children into the flames.

The Roman Senate had already decided that Carthage would be destroyed. The decision was not Scipio's to make, though some ancient accounts suggest he felt the weight of what he was witnessing, as a great city was being wiped from existence. Whatever his private feelings, the orders were carried out. Much of the population was sold into slavery. An enormous amount of plunder went to Rome. The territory became the

Roman province of Africa (Africa Proconsularis), while other areas were designated *ager publicus* ("public land"), with the local population required to pay tribute. The Numidian kingdom, under Masinissa's sons, expanded into the surrounding lands. Masinissa himself had died during the war at an extreme old age. He was thought to be around ninety, which meant he had outlived almost everyone from the generation that fought Hannibal.

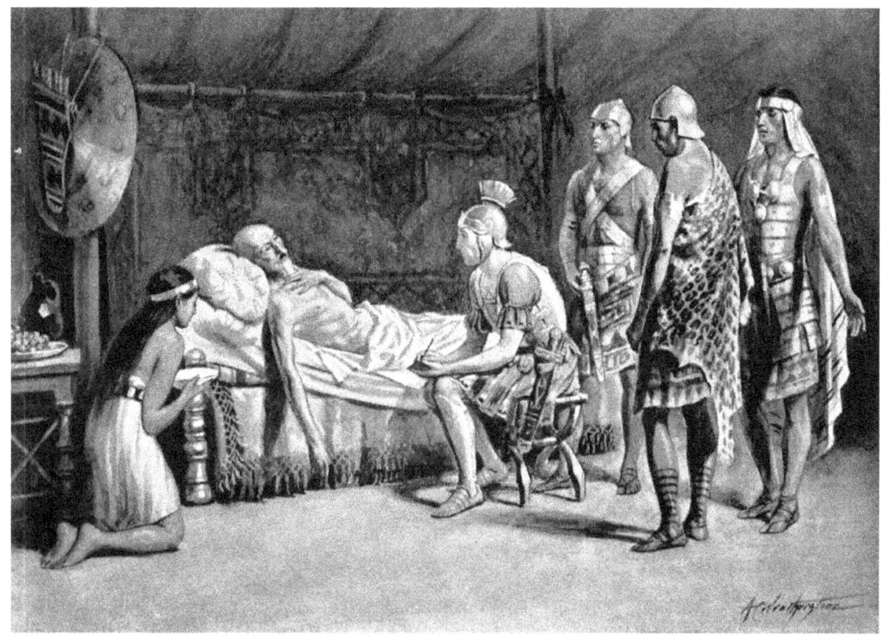

Scipio at the deathbed of Masinissa, by Alfred C. Weatherstone.[10]

What the destruction of Carthage demonstrated was not simply that Rome could win a siege. It showed the extent to which Roman military and political dominance had become total in the Mediterranean world. Carthage had rebuilt itself from the ruins of the Second Punic War, recovering its wealth and trade networks. It had survived fifty years of Roman pressure and Numidian harassment, and it still was not enough. The city that had once sent Hannibal to the gates of Rome was gone. Scipio Aemilianus received the title Africanus Minor in recognition of the victory, distinguishing him from Scipio Africanus, the general who had won at Zama a lifetime before.

Rome had started as a city on the Tiber surrounded by hostile neighbors. It had spent two centuries fighting for Italy, then another century fighting for the Mediterranean. Now, there was no serious rival left in the west. The next chapter was already beginning.

Lands owned by the Romans after the Third Punic War[11]

Chapter 4: Marius and the Professionalization of the Legions

The difficulties facing the Roman army in the 2nd century BCE were bound up with social and economic changes that had been building for generations. As Rome expanded rapidly and warfare grew more expensive, small farmers struggled to maintain their property during long military campaigns. They were away for years at a time, and their land was worked poorly or not at all. An influx of slaves gave wealthy landowners cheap labor for their great estates, known as the latifundia, and the small farming class could not compete with that. The pool of property-holding citizens eligible for conscription may have been shrinking as a result, and the traditional citizen militia was straining to keep pace with the demands being placed on it. Meanwhile, expansion kept requiring more men. The pressure on an already stressed system kept building.

Reform efforts intensified under the Gracchi brothers, particularly with Tiberius Gracchus in 133 BCE. He proposed redistributing public land (ager publicus) that had been illegally occupied by wealthy elites, returning it to landless Roman citizens and, in theory, rebuilding the class of small farmers who formed the backbone of the army. The program was implemented, but many recipients later struggled to maintain their farms under the same economic pressures that had dispossessed people in the first place. The economic instability affecting both the army and the state created fertile ground for corruption and bribery, which further eroded confidence in Roman institutions. The sluggishness of the military response to Rome's problems and the inability to wage wars effectively frustrated Roman society, none more so than the men who actually had to fight them.

One of those men was Gaius Marius, born in 157 BCE. He was a *homo novus*, which means he had no family connections or inherited status. He earned everything himself. He took to military life early and gained distinction as a young soldier under Scipio Aemilianus during the siege of Numantia in 134 BCE. He later served as a military tribune, and after a failed attempt at a magistracy, he worked his way up to quaestor. He was elected tribune of the plebs in 119 BCE. His social standing was modest, but it improved considerably when he married the young Julia, from the noble Julian family, a connection that would take on significance long after Marius himself was gone.

A potential bust of Marius[12]

His chance at something larger came through a crisis in Numidia. After Masinissa's death in 149 BCE, his kingdom was divided among his three sons: Micipsa, Gulussa, and Mastanabal. Gulussa and Mastanabal eventually died, leaving Micipsa to rule alone. Into this situation stepped Jugurtha, the illegitimate son of Mastanabal. He was ambitious and shrewd, and he had spent time on campaign in Spain watching how the Romans operated, including how Roman officials could be bought.

Micipsa adopted Jugurtha and made him co-heir alongside his own sons, hoping to manage the situation. It didn't work. After Micipsa's death in 118 BCE, Jugurtha employed treachery, assassination, and well-placed bribes to consolidate power. Rome intervened and divided Numidia between Jugurtha and his rival Adherbal following their civil war, giving Jugurtha the western portion. That arrangement lasted only as long as Jugurtha let it.

In Rome, it soon emerged that Jugurtha had bribed numerous officials and even consuls to secure favorable outcomes in the negotiations. The observation he reportedly made about the city, recorded by Sallust, a historian from the Roman Republic, captured what he had concluded from all of it. "[It is] a city for sale and doomed to speedy destruction if it finds a purchaser."[i]

Despite the treaty, Jugurtha quickly attacked the eastern part of Numidia, forcing Rome's hand. The war that followed exposed everything that was wrong with the Roman military establishment at the time. Multiple commanders tried and failed to pin Jugurtha down. He was a gifted guerrilla fighter, and he understood the terrain. He also continued to exploit Roman corruption wherever he found it, which was frequently. The war dragged on far longer than it should have.

Marius served in the campaign as a legate under Consul Quintus Caecilius Metellus. Whatever friction existed between the two men personally—and accounts suggest there was real tension—Marius's abilities were impossible to ignore. He shared meals with his soldiers and worked alongside them, and they respected him for it. In 107 BCE, he was elected consul, a victory seen by many as a rebuke of the corrupt oligarchy that had mismanaged the war. He took over the campaign and, with it, jurisdiction over Metellus's troops.

Marius made real progress where his predecessors had not, but Jugurtha's evasiveness remained a problem. The final solution came through his quaestor, Lucius Cornelius Sulla. Sulla negotiated with Bocchus I of Mauretania, Jugurtha's own father-in-law, who ultimately betrayed Jugurtha and handed him over to the Romans. It was a diplomatic coup as much as a military one, and the feat belonged to

[i] Sallust, *The Jugurthine War and the Conspiracy of Catiline*, Roman Roads Media, 2015, p.29.

Sulla–a fact that would sit uneasily between the two men for years afterward.

The capture of Jugurtha[13]

Jugurtha was captured in 105 BCE and paraded in chains through Rome during Marius's triumph. He was then taken to the Tullianum prison and executed in 104 BCE. Ancient sources say strangulation was the method. The Jugurthine War was over after nearly a decade.

What the war left behind mattered as much as its outcome. Jugurtha had not won, but he had succeeded in exposing the rot in the Roman system: the corruption, the favoritism, the willingness of officials to be bought, and the failures of an army structure that had not kept pace with the demands of an empire. Rome had won, but it didn't come out with a great image. The pressure for serious military reform was building, and Marius was the man in the right position to deliver it.

A new threat was already forming on Rome's northern borders. The Cimbri and Teutones, northern tribal groups, had been on the move for years. Their migration stalled when they reached the Balkans, where local resistance pushed them westward and eventually toward Italy's borders. They asked for land within Roman territory in exchange for military submission. The Senate refused, as rulers before them had. That refusal set off a chain of conflicts that Rome handled badly, one after another.

At Noreia in 113 BCE and then, far worse, at Arausio in 105 BCE, the Roman forces were destroyed. At Arausio, tens of thousands of soldiers were lost. The scale of it was shocking even by Roman standards. General after general was sent north and failed. The road into Italy was open, but the tribes had not yet taken it. Why they didn't remains unclear. They turned toward Spain and Gaul instead, which gave Rome the time it badly needed.

The Cimbri are often associated with the Jutland Peninsula, though their exact origins are debated. What is certain is that the migrating tribes had been gathering followers as they moved. Other groups had been absorbed or joined along the way. Ancient sources give figures of up to 200,000 warriors, but modern historians treat those numbers with serious skepticism. The force was large, but it is impossible to say how large.

After his success in Africa, Marius was repeatedly elected consul and given command against the northern tribes. This was an extraordinary concentration of power in one man, but it was justified by the severity of the threat. He used the time before the battle to train and reorganize his forces, preparing them for a kind of warfare that was very different from the desert campaigns against Jugurtha.

The tribes eventually moved into southern Gaul. Marius followed, building fortifications along the route and fighting off their probing attacks without committing to a full engagement. He was waiting. The battle came unexpectedly at first. A detachment of Roman allies, Ligurians, stumbled on the Ambrones bathing in a river, and fighting broke out before any plan had been made. Marius threw his legions in. The Ambrones were beaten, but the Teutones were still in the hills nearby.

A few days passed. Marius drew his army into battle order on high ground near Aquae Sextiae in what is now southern France. The tribes attacked uphill and were driven back. When they broke and fled, Marcus Claudius Marcellus was waiting in the woods with around three thousand men. He hit them from behind. The slaughter was severe. Later accounts claimed the soil around Aquae Sextiae produced exceptional harvests for years afterward, enriched by the dead. Whether that is true or an embellishment, the battle was a decisive Roman victory.

The Cimbri were still coming, though. Their indecision about when and where to strike gave Marius time to move east and link up with his co-commander, Quintus Lutatius Catulus. The final confrontation came at Vercellae in northern Italy. Boiorix, a leader of the Cimbri, had apparently arranged the time and place with Marius in advance; it would be a formal pitched battle rather than a running fight. Marius positioned his troops so the morning sun was at their backs and in the eyes of the enemy, a small advantage that mattered.

The tribes, reportedly as many as 150,000 strong (though again, ancient numbers should be treated cautiously), advanced and were met with a Roman charge. The battlefield filled with dust. In the chaos, Marius misjudged his own advance and missed the main body of the enemy entirely. It was Catulus, with around twenty thousand men and Sulla leading the cavalry, who absorbed and broke the Cimbrian assault. Exhausted by the summer heat and ground down by tight Roman formations, the tribal warriors collapsed. The battle ended the threat to Rome's northern frontier.

Marius and Catulus shared a triumph, but popular opinion credited Marius as the man who had saved Italy, which irritated Catulus. It likely irritated Sulla too, who had done the hardest fighting at Vercellae.

What Marius had been doing with the army throughout this period was significant. The changes he introduced or that are traditionally associated with him—modern historians debate how systematic or deliberate they were—led to a fundamental shift in how Rome waged war. They built on earlier reform efforts going back to the Gracchi brothers, but they went considerably further.

Before Marius, the army still reflected, at least in theory, the old Servian class structure. Property-owning citizens were organized by wealth, with each providing their own equipment. That model had been showing cracks for decades. Long overseas campaigns were hard for men who had farms to return to, and the pool of eligible citizens may have been shrinking. Marius's changes, beginning after his election as consul in 107

BCE, moved away from that model. Landless citizens, the *capite censi*, those counted by head rather than by property, became eligible to serve. Soldiers were paid a regular wage, the *stipendium*, and military service became a career rather than a civic obligation with a defined end.

Changes in equipment and organization followed. The old distinctions between different grades of infantry, such as the varying arms and armor of different property classes, gave way to something more uniform. All legionaries carried the pilum (javelin) and gladius (sword), wore mail armor and a bronze helmet, and carried a long oval shield. They trained intensively in close-quarters weapons drills. The five old legion standards—a boar, a wolf, a horse, an eagle, and a Minotaur—were replaced with a single silver eagle, the aquila. These men now had a shared identity, similar equipment, and a shared symbol. The esprit de corps that developed was something the old property-based militia had never really had.[i]

The aquila, the symbol of the legion[14]

Cavalry and light infantry (the velites) were increasingly filled by allied and auxiliary troops rather than drawn from the citizen legion itself. The standard auxiliary cavalry unit was the ala, a regiment of around five hundred horsemen, while infantry auxilia were organized into cohorts of a similar size. The primary tactical unit shifted from the maniple to the cohort. A legion's ten cohorts gave the army a flexible building block suited for the varied terrain and enemies Rome was now fighting across the Mediterranean world.

[i] Esprit de corps is a French phrase meaning cohesion or a common spirit existing in the members of a group, inspiring devotion to a mutual goal.

The logistics changed too. The reforms associated with Marius reduced the size of the baggage train, the *impedimenta*, by requiring soldiers to carry more of their own gear. This gave rise to the nickname "Marius's mules," a term for soldiers loaded down with their own equipment. Soldiers had to carry tools for earthworks, including a sickle and a dolabra (pickaxe), cooking utensils, two wooden stakes for field fortifications, a blanket, a coat, and several days' worth of rations. Cattle accompanied the column carrying the heaviest items, mainly the tents and bulk supplies, but the soldiers themselves carried a great deal more than before. The army moved faster because of it.

Among the tactical formations developed in this period was the testudo, the tortoise. Legionaries locked their large shields overhead and around the edges of the formation, creating a shell of overlapping wood and iron that protected against missiles from above. It was slow and cumbersome, but the formation was almost impervious to arrows and stones. When the time came, it could open, and the men inside could charge. It was the kind of disciplined collective maneuver that only a well-trained, cohesive force could execute under fire.

The political consequences of all this were harder to see at the time, although they are obvious in retrospect. When soldiers serve long terms, are paid by their commanders, and depend on those commanders for land grants after being discharged, their loyalty goes to the man rather than the institution. Lucius Appuleius Saturninus, a populist tribune and ally of Marius, pushed legislation through to provide land settlements for Marius's veterans, using violence and intimidation to get it done. In 100 BCE, Saturninus's supporters arranged the murder of a rival candidate. Street violence spread. The Senate invoked the *senatus consultum ultimum* and called on Marius—of all people—to restore order against his own ally. He did it. Saturninus was forced to surrender and took refuge in the Senate building, where a mob got to him anyway.

What that episode revealed was that armed men loyal to a particular general were now a force in Roman politics. As Sallust put it, a soldier "has no regard for his property, having none, and considers anything honorable for which he receives pay."[i] These men were seen as disposable, but they were obedient and grateful to whoever controlled their wages and futures. The veterans were a political bloc. They could be used to gain influence.

---

[i] Sallust, *The Jugurthine War and the Conspiracy of Catiline*, Roman Roads Media, 2015.

The volunteers who filled the new army also gained something beyond pay. Roman citizenship had been extended to many Italian allies, though full citizenship across the peninsula came only after the Social War of 91–88 BCE, and military service was one route into that status. The landless poor could gain wealth, land, and standing in ways that had previously been closed to them. Traditional aristocratic families found their grip on power loosening as men like Marius (*novi homines*, new men without ancient lineage) rose through military achievement.

The first civil war grew out of this transformation. Marius and Lucius Cornelius Sulla had been circling each other since the Jugurthine War, when Sulla's role in capturing Jugurtha had created a tension between them that had never been fully resolved. The flashpoint came over command of the Mithridatic War in 88 BCE. Sulla had been awarded the command as consul. Marius maneuvered to have it transferred to himself. Sulla's soldiers, who were loyal to him, not to the state, feared being replaced by Marius's men. Sulla used that loyalty to do something that had never been done before. He marched his army on Rome itself. Marius fled, and the city fell to Sulla without serious resistance. It was the first time in Roman history that a general had seized power by force of arms.

Sulla set a template. One of the consuls, Cornelius Cinna, later joined with Marius's veterans and retook Rome. The Greek historian Appian's account of what followed is stark. Soldiers "killed remorselessly, and severed the necks of men already dead, parading horrors before the public eye, either to inspire fear and terror, or for a monstrous spectacle."[i]

The Senate had been losing credibility since the Jugurthine War, when Roman nobles had taken Jugurtha's bribes openly. That damage had never been repaired. What Marius set in motion and what Sulla demonstrated could be done was that the army could override the Senate entirely. Pompey and Caesar would both use the lesson. The normalization of armed force as a tool of internal politics contributed to the eventual collapse of the Roman Republic, a process that played out over the following decades. Whether it was inevitable is another question. What is clear is that once Sulla marched on Rome, the rules had changed, and everyone knew it.

[i] Appian, *The Histories,* Loeb Classical Library, 1913.

Chapter 5: Caesar's Gallic Campaigns

Sculpture of Julius Caesar.[15]

Between them, Marius and Sulla broke something that couldn't be fixed. The legions had stopped being Rome's army in any meaningful sense; they were the general's army, loyal to whoever paid them and promised them land when it was over. Once that happened, everything else was a matter of time.

Sulla saw it clearly enough. So did Marius and, later, Caesar. What all three understood, and what the Senate kept failing to grasp until it was too late, was that supreme power in Rome had a prerequisite. One had to be the best general first. The magistracy, the traditions, the centuries of carefully managed institutional power all meant nothing if someone marched an army through the gates. Marius and Sulla had proved that. Caesar just used the proof.

Caesar's connection to Marius was through marriage. Marius had married Julia, who was Caesar's aunt, which made Caesar Marius's nephew. When Sulla consolidated power in 82 BCE, Caesar's family connections made him suspect. As the nephew of Marius by marriage and the son-in-law of Cinna, he represented the faction Sulla had just defeated. Sulla stripped him of the Flamen Dialis, the priesthood of Jupiter, one of the oldest religious offices in Rome. However, he let him live, which turned out to be the most consequential act of mercy in Roman history.

Caesar survived and eventually escaped Rome, crossing into Asia to serve under the praetor Marcus Minucius Thermus. Away from Sulla's orbit, he started building the thing he actually needed: a reputation. He fought at the siege of Mytilene in 81 BCE on the island of Lesbos, where he distinguished himself enough to be awarded the *corona civica* (the civic crown). He had saved the life of a Roman citizen in battle, and back in Rome, this entitled him to public honors that money couldn't buy. He moved on to Cilicia, serving under Publius Servilius Vatia Isauricus. When Sulla died in 78 BCE, Caesar returned to Rome to begin his political career.

What followed was years of grinding political work. The *cursus honorum*, the fixed ladder of Roman offices, didn't bend for ambition, at least not openly anyway. Caesar spent decades climbing this political ladder. He became a military tribune around 72 BCE, quaestor in 69 BCE, and aedile in 65 BCE. Then, in 63 BCE, he won election as pontifex maximus, making him chief priest of Rome, the senior religious office in the state. He beat out candidates who were far more senior than himself. He became praetor in 62 BCE and then consul in 59 BCE.

The consulship itself was not the real prize, as it only lasted a year. What Caesar wanted was what came after. A proconsular command meant an army, a province, and time. Securing it required backing, which led to his famous alliance with Pompey and Crassus, known as the First Triumvirate. Pompey was the most celebrated general of the age, and Crassus was one of the wealthiest men in Rome. With their support, Caesar obtained command of Cisalpine Gaul and Illyricum, with Transalpine Gaul added shortly after, beginning in 58 BCE. The command was granted for five years initially, but it was extended in 55 BCE.

What Caesar did with this command is documented in his own words. The *Commentarii de Bello Gallico,* his account of the Gallic Wars, is a detailed military record written in the third person. It is both history and self-promotion. The campaigns ran from 58 BCE to around 50 BCE, primarily covering what is now France, Belgium, and Switzerland. Caesar crossed the Rhine into Germanic territory and landed twice in Britain. The wars built his reputation, filled his war chest with plunder, and gave him the veteran army he would later need for something more ambitious.

Setting the Scene

In 58 BCE, when Caesar took up his command in Gaul, the Roman Republic controlled Hispania, Italia, the Adriatic coast from Istria through the Roman provinces of Macedonia and Achaea in Greece, parts of Asia Minor, parts of Syria and Judea, Cyprus, and the Roman province of Africa (roughly modern Tunisia). A large part of Gaul remained outside Roman control. Caesar was about to change that.

Caesar opens his account by laying out the political geography of the region. The Gauls, members of the broader Celtic grouping of peoples, inhabited roughly modern-day France, Belgium, Switzerland, and parts of northern Italy before the Roman conquest. Caesar divided them into distinct factions and treated each one accordingly. His first focus was the Helvetii, who occupied what is now Switzerland. Around the time Caesar took up his proconsulship, the Helvetii had resolved to migrate westward into Gaul, led by a chieftain named Orgetorix. They burned twelve towns and around four hundred villages behind them to prevent any possibility of turning back. They also gathered neighboring tribes on their move toward western Gaul, attempting to pass through Roman territory near Lake Geneva.

Caesar was not going to allow it. He ordered the construction of a defensive line of trenches and walls stretching from Lake Geneva to the Jura Mountains, roughly nineteen Roman miles in total. While that was being built, he was already working the diplomatic angle, maintaining contact with the Gallic tribes nearest to the Helvetii, namely the Aedui, Sequani, and Santones. These two things together—the capacity to organize large-scale military engineering at speed and the ability to exploit rivalries between Gallic tribes, a strategy often described as "divide and conquer"—were as central to Caesar's success as any battle he fought.

He was a tireless operator. Throughout his years in Gaul, Caesar was constantly in motion, inspecting fortifications, overseeing engagements, negotiating with tribal leaders, and traveling back to Italy to raise fresh legions. Somehow, he also found time to write or dictate the *Commentarii de Bello Gallico*, manage his relationships with Pompey and Crassus back in Rome, and keep a close eye on the political situation in the capital. He was capable of considerable ruthlessness when the situation called for it. The *Commentarii* are full of accounts, told in Caesar's own prose, of massacres and enslavements of Gallic populations.

When it suited him, Caesar was equally capable of framing military action in the language of Roman honor and ancestral obligation. After defeating a portion of the Helvetii, he wrote, "Thus, whether by chance, or by the design of the immortal gods, that part of the Helvetian state which had brought a signal calamity upon the Roman people, was the first to pay the penalty. In this Caesar avenged not only the public but also his own personal wrongs, because the Tigurini had slain Lucius Piso, the lieutenant [of Cassius], the grandfather of Lucius Calpurnius Piso, his [Caesar's] father-in-law, in the same battle as Cassius himself."[i]

The passage is a useful window into how Caesar operated. Caesar was framing a military victory as an act of personal and civic vengeance; the state had been wronged, and so had his family. The two conveniently pointed in the same direction. He was not a hypocrite in any simple sense, but he was also a man who understood that invoking them at the right moment was useful. Caesar's actions played a major role in the collapse of the Roman Republic, and at several points, he faced a choice between his own advancement and the survival of Republican institutions. He chose himself.

But we are getting slightly ahead of the story. The Gallic Wars themselves reveal Caesar's character more clearly than any summary can, and several of their key episodes are worth examining in detail.

Campaigns Against the Tribes

The Helvetii were quite possibly never a genuine threat to the Roman Republic, but Caesar moved against them anyway. They had been heading westward toward the Saône River, and Caesar's forces caught them mid-crossing. The Tigurini, a subgroup of the Helvetii still waiting on the eastern bank, were destroyed. The rest pushed on, and Caesar followed.

After dealing with the Tigurini, Caesar moved his troops across the Saône to keep pace with the main Helvetii force. The two armies entered the territory of the Aedui, who were nominally Roman allies, although reluctantly so. Caesar soon uncovered intrigue among the Aedui that was undermining the campaign. Dumnorix, the brother of the pro-Roman

---

[i] Caesar, Julius, *Commentarii De Bello Gallico*, W. J. Gage & Co., 1890, p.7

noble Diviciacus, was implicated in the affair and was accused of working against Caesar's interests as the campaign progressed. Curiously, Caesar allowed him to live, keeping him under close watch rather than making an example of him, largely out of respect for Diviciacus, who remained loyal.

The Romans followed the Helvetii without a decisive engagement for some time. Roman provisions started to run low, and Caesar began looking toward Bibracte, the Aedui capital, about twenty miles away, as a supply source. The Helvetii got wind of this and turned to pursue the Romans, intending, as Caesar puts it, to "annoy our men in the rear."[i] It is a small detail, but an illuminating one. Modern readers tend to picture ancient warfare as a sequence of grand set-piece battles, with two armies crashing into each other on an open plain. In reality, it was messier and slower. There would be weeks of marching, digging, following the enemy, camping, breaking camp, skirmishing, provoking, and waiting, punctuated occasionally by something that could be called a real battle.

Caesar saw that the Helvetii were growing bolder and looking for an open engagement. He moved his forces to higher ground and arranged them in multiple lines. Then—and he records this himself—he dismounted his horse and ordered his officers to do the same. The message to his men was deliberate. Nobody with a horse was going anywhere. Officers and commanders would fight on foot alongside the rest.

The Helvetii approached. The Romans threw their javelins. This was standard Roman practice, and the pilum was designed with it in mind. Even when it failed to wound or kill, the heavy javelin tended to lodge in an enemy's shield, making it unwieldy and nearly impossible to use. Many Helvetii threw their shields away rather than try to fight encumbered by a javelin shaft. This left them exposed.

The Helvetii began falling back toward a nearby hill where reinforcements were waiting. As the Romans pressed the pursuit uphill, those reinforcements hit them from behind. The Roman force split, with one part facing upward and another part turning to meet the new attack from the rear. The fighting went on into the evening before the Helvetii finally gave way.

After a few days of recovery, Caesar resumed the pursuit. The Helvetii eventually sent envoys to ask for terms. Caesar took hostages and weapons, then ordered them back to their original territory (modern

---

[i] Caesar, Julius, *Commentarii De Bello Gallico*, W. J. Gage & Co., 1890, p. 13

Switzerland). His reasoning, as he explains it, was that the Helvetii served as a buffer against the Germanic peoples to the east, whom Caesar regarded as a threat in their own right. He also recorded figures he claims were found inscribed in Greek on Helvetii territory: 263,000 Helvetii, 36,000 Tulingi, 14,000 Latobrigii, 23,000 Rauraci, and 32,000 Boii. There were 368,000 in total, of whom 92,000 were fighters. Only 110,000 survived by Caesar's count. Caesar likely exaggerated these figures considerably; most modern estimates put the total number of migrants at 150,000 or fewer.

Rome recognized Ariovistus, the king of the Suebi, as a friend and ally of the Roman people. However, in 59 BCE, reports arrived that a hundred Suebi clans were attempting to cross the Rhine into Gaul. Caesar had his justification. The Romans had clashed with Germanic peoples before—the Cimbrian War had happened just a generation earlier—but this was a direct confrontation over control of the Rhine frontier.

In 58 BCE, Caesar moved against Ariovistus. The two forces met somewhere in Upper Alsace near the Rhine. Negotiations failed, and skirmishes between the camps grew more frequent. Ariovistus established a second camp that threatened Roman supply and foraging routes. Facing mounting pressure, Caesar attacked with his six legions and supporting auxiliaries. According to Caesar, the majority of Ariovistus's force, which he puts at 120,000 (a number that is almost certainly inflated), was destroyed. Ariovistus crossed back over the Rhine with a handful of survivors and was not a factor again. Two major threats, the Helvetii and Ariovistus's Germanic coalition, had been dealt with in a single campaigning season. Caesar was well positioned to push further.

His victories in 58 BCE alarmed the tribes of the north. The following year, Caesar marched against the Belgic confederation, which controlled what is now Belgium. Caesar describes them as the fiercest of the Gauls, hardened by constant conflict with the Germanic tribes across the Rhine and, as he notes pointedly, were less exposed to the softening influence of Roman trade and culture. The Belgic coalition put forward various tribal contingents. Caesar claims there were around 288,000 warriors in total, a figure modern historians treat skeptically. Large parts of the confederation submitted without serious resistance as Caesar advanced. The Suessiones, Bellovaci, and Ambiani gave way as he entered their territory. However, the Nervii, along with the Atrebates, Atuatuci, and Viromandui, chose to fight.

At the Battle of the Sabis, Caesar came close to a serious defeat. The Nervii hit the Romans while they were still making camp, catching them before they could form proper battle order. It was one of the most dangerous moments of the entire Gallic campaign. It was resolved only by Caesar's personal intervention on the field and the arrival of reinforcements.

The Atuatuci initially sued for peace and surrendered their weapons—or at least, they appeared to. They had concealed part of their arsenal during the handover. That night, they launched a sortie from the city walls under the cover of darkness, attacking the Roman positions outside. The Romans drove them back. Caesar was not lenient. He had fifty-three thousand of them sold into slavery.

After this, most of the Belgic tribes accepted Roman authority, at least nominally. During the following winter, the Gauls were required to provide grain for Roman troops. In 56 BCE, the Veneti of the northwestern coast rebelled, seizing Roman officials who had been sent to requisition supplies. They had been preparing. Their villages were fortified, positioned on coastal promontories that the tide made nearly inaccessible, and their fleet was built for Atlantic conditions. These were heavy, high-sided vessels with leather sails, suited for rough northern waters in a way that Roman Mediterranean ships were not.

Caesar recognized the problem and appointed Decimus Junius Brutus to build and lead a new fleet. When the two navies met off the Brittany coast, the Romans found a solution to the Venetis' stronger hulls. They used hooked blades on long poles to cut the Veneti rigging, disabling their sails and leaving the heavy vessels unable to maneuver. Without wind, the Veneti ships were helpless, and the Romans picked them off.

On land and without their fleet, the Veneti had no advantage. They surrendered. Caesar executed the tribal elders and enslaved much of the population. He moved against the Morini and Menapii tribes along the coast next, but thick forests and difficult terrain stopped the Roman advance. He let them go.

Attention then shifted to the Rhine. Germanic tribes, the Usipetes and Tencteri, had been driven out of their territory by the Suebi and were attempting to cross into Gaul. Caesar refused their request to settle there. A cavalry engagement followed, in which a Germanic force of around eight hundred horsemen defeated a Roman unit of five thousand. It was an embarrassing defeat. Caesar responded by attacking their camp, killing large numbers of men, women, and children in the process. He claims the dead numbered in the hundreds of thousands. The figure is almost certainly inflated propaganda, but the violence was real and deliberate.

To demonstrate Roman reach, Caesar had his engineers build a bridge across the Rhine in ten days in 55 BCE. The troops crossed, made a show of force in Germanic territory, and returned. The bridge was then destroyed. Caesar did not intend for there to be a conquest; he meant for it to be a statement. Germanic tribes would not find safety simply by crossing the river.

At a meeting of the First Triumvirate known as the Luca Conference, Caesar secured another five years as governor. Pompey and Crassus took the consulship for 55 BCE. With his position secured, Caesar turned to something no Roman commander had attempted: Britain. The island was little known to the Mediterranean world. It was distant, but it had been providing refuge to Gallic leaders who escaped Roman control.

His first attempt, in 55 BCE, was forced back almost immediately by bad weather and the difficulty of landing on an open coast. However, the political effect in Rome was considerable. The Roman public was taken with the idea of armies crossing the ocean. The following year, Caesar returned with a far larger force. He claims he led eight hundred ships of various types. The scale of it was enough that the Britons did not contest the landing. Caesar left Quintus Atrius at the coast with a holding force and pushed inland, extracting tribute from several tribal leaders and installing client kings. Then bad weather struck again, damaging the fleet significantly, and the troops were pulled back to repair it. Caesar withdrew before winter without leaving any permanent garrison.

Britain was not conquered. However, it had been entered, its tribes had formally acknowledged Roman power (even if the tribute they promised was largely theoretical, as no record exists of it actually being paid), and Caesar had stopped British support from reaching the Gauls. More practically, he had added another extraordinary episode to the account he was building of his own campaigns.

A standard bearer of the Tenth Legion leading the Romans to a beach in England[16]

Unrest in Gaul

Crop failures in 54 BCE hit both sides hard. The Gauls were already living under the pressure of Roman occupation, and the food shortage pushed resentment into something more organized. A common cause was taking shape.

The Eburones tribe, under Ambiorix, moved first. He approached Caesar's legate, Quintus Titurius Sabinus, with a warning. Germanic tribes were massing to invade Gaul, and the whole region was on the verge of revolt. If the Romans abandoned their camp and marched out, Ambiorix offered safe passage.

Sabinus believed him. He and his co-commander, Lucius Aurunculeius Cotta, led their men out. However, it was a ploy. They were ambushed in a narrow valley, and both commanders died. Most of the force died too.

The news spread fast. The Nervii, Atuatuci, and other tribes read Sabinus's and Cotta's destruction as a signal and moved against the nearest Roman positions. A force that Caesar puts at around sixty thousand (probably an exaggeration, but it was still large) laid siege to the camp of Quintus Tullius Cicero, brother of the famous orator Marcus Tullius Cicero. The Gauls had learned something about Roman siege methods, partly from watching and partly from Roman prisoners, and they put that knowledge to use. The siege lasted for two weeks.

Caesar, who was still in Gaul, got word and moved quickly, sending two legions to break it. He relieved Quintus Cicero's camp and scattered the attackers. The camp held. Caesar's admiration for Quintus Cicero's conduct during the siege was genuine, as he says so directly in his accounts.

The winter had been brutal, the revolt had been dangerous, and the mood in the Roman command was not good even after the immediate threat was contained. Caesar's response was to go on the offensive. He launched a broad punitive campaign against Ambiorix and the Eburones. He wanted to make an example of them to discourage anything similar from happening again.

It did not fully work. Gallic anxiety and resentment kept building. In 52 BCE, it produced something the Romans had not yet faced in Gaul: a unified, coordinated uprising across multiple tribes, with a single capable leader holding it together.

That leader was Vercingetorix, a young Arvernian nobleman with enough charisma and political skill to assemble a coalition that would normally have been impossible. The Gallic tribes had spent as much of their history fighting each other as fighting anyone else. Getting them to act together required something, and Vercingetorix managed it during the winter of 53–52 BCE. Caesar was in Cisalpine Gaul when he heard about the alliance and moved north immediately.

Vercingetorix fought the war logically, at least at first. He avoided open engagement with Roman legions, concentrated on cutting supply lines and harassing foraging parties, and abandoned towns he judged indefensible rather than lose men trying to hold them. The strategy was sound. The Romans were strong in pitched battles and sieges. If Vercingetorix could keep them hungry and on the move, then he had a chance.

It broke down at Avaricum. The inhabitants refused to burn their own city (one of the most beautiful in Gaul, by Caesar's account), and

Vercingetorix reluctantly agreed to defend it. Caesar besieged it in difficult conditions, and the Romans took it. The population was massacred. Vercingetorix's strategic instinct had been right, but he had given in to political pressure and paid for it. Remarkably, the coalition held together anyway. His authority survived the defeat.

The decisive moment came at Alesia. Vercingetorix had gathered a large force. Caesar estimates around eighty thousand men in the town itself, and there was a relief army that he says was much larger, though both figures are probably inflated. Vercingetorix then fortified the hilltop position. Caesar did what Caesar did: he built. The Romans constructed a double ring of circumvallation around the entire hill, miles of fortifications facing both inward toward Alesia and outward toward the relief force that was coming.[i] When the relief army arrived and attacked from outside while the defenders struck from within, Caesar's men held both lines simultaneously. The relief force was broken. The garrison had no way out and nothing left to eat.

Vercingetorix throws down his arms at the feet of Julius Caesar by Lionel Royer[17]

Vercingetorix was forced to surrender. He rode out of Alesia in full armor, circled Caesar's position, and dismounted. Caesar held him for six years before bringing him to Rome. He was paraded through the city

[i] Circumvallation is a military tactic that involves building a continuous line of fortified, earthen ramparts and trenches surrounding the besieged city.

during Caesar's triumph and executed at the Tullianum prison in 46 BCE.

After Alesia, organized Gallic resistance collapsed. The remaining tribes submitted one by one, and by 50 BCE, Caesar's conquest was effectively complete. Of course, the term "complete" is relative. Caesar had subdued most of Gaul between 58 and 50 BCE, but resistance never fully disappeared. Roman consolidation of the region continued long after he left.

Outside of Caesar's own *Commentarii de Bello Gallico,* which, as you can see, should be read with skepticism, given that Caesar was both the author and the subject, almost no written sources survive for the Gallic Wars. The Gauls kept no written records. Whatever the conflict looked like from their side is gone.

As for Caesar himself, the *Commentarii* reveal a commander who says relatively little about his own physical role in combat. He was present, he was exposed to danger, and he led from the front, but he describes himself as directing and encouraging rather than fighting. Whether that reflects modesty or is simply an accurate self-assessment is hard to say.

In eight years, Caesar had transformed the northwest of the known world. The cultural and political consequences of Roman rule in Gaul lasted for centuries, shaping language, law, and administration across what is now France, Belgium, and beyond.

However, the conquest of Gaul was never really the endpoint. Caesar's command was expiring, his enemies in the Senate were waiting, and the legal protection that his proconsulship had provided was about to disappear. Stripped of his army, he would be a private citizen facing prosecution.

In January 49 BCE, he made a decision that changed everything. He led his Thirteenth Legion across the Rubicon, the river that marked the boundary between his province and Italy proper. Roman law explicitly forbade any general from performing such an act under arms. It was, in effect, a declaration of war against the Senate and the Roman Republic.

Pompey, now Caesar's main rival and the Senate's chosen defender, fled Italy almost immediately. Caesar swept down the peninsula in a matter of weeks, meeting almost no resistance. The civil war that followed lasted four years and took the conflict across the entire Mediterranean world. Caesar won all of it. By 45 BCE, he was back in Rome, where he was appointed dictator perpetuo (dictator in perpetuity), a title with no precedent and no defined end.

The Roman Republic still had a form, but there was not much substance. Caesar held the power, and he showed little interest in pretending otherwise. His military dominance, his concentration of power, and his apparent indifference to Republican tradition drove others to act.

On the Ides of March, 44 BCE, roughly eighty senators and associates, among them Gaius Cassius Longinus and Marcus Junius Brutus, a man Caesar had treated as a close friend and by some accounts something more, surrounded and stabbed him. He was stabbed twenty-three times. His assassins scattered after the attack.

Whether Caesar said anything at the end, and what it might have been, is unknown. The line "Et tu, Brute?" ("You too, Brutus?") comes from Shakespeare's play, which was written sixteen centuries later and has no basis in any contemporary account. It stuck anyway, the way things do when they capture something that feels emotionally true even if it isn't historically real. Whether the assassination was an act of principle or done out of fear or ambition depends on which conspirator you're talking about. What it produced, though, was a power vacuum, and the man who filled it was Octavian.

Chapter 6: Augustus and the Imperial Army

In the wake of Julius Caesar's assassination on March 15th, 44 BCE, chaos gripped the ailing Roman Republic as Caesar's assassins, known as the Liberators, failed to consolidate their hold on Rome and to subdue the pro-Caesar faction, the leadership of which was seized by Caesar's lieutenant Marcus Antonius (commonly known as Mark Antony). Cicero (the famous orator, not the military leader) and the Senate attempted to restrain Antony through political pressure, but the situation was already too far gone for rhetoric, such as Cicero's *Philippics,* to hold. More pressing was the fact that Antony was not Caesar's chosen successor. In his last will

Augustus of Prima Porta[18]

and testament, Caesar adopted his eighteen-year-old grand-nephew, Gaius Octavius, as his son and legal heir.

Gaius Octavius (also known as Octavian, later Augustus) was not an obvious choice for a successor. He came from a wealthy equestrian family, so his lineage was respectable but not part of the old senatorial elite. Octavian had only limited military experience, having served with Caesar in Spain, and was only distantly related to Caesar. However, he did share his grand-uncle's cunning and political acumen, and he was quick to establish himself as Caesar's heir.

Caesar's supporters and, crucially, Caesar's veteran legions came to his side. He also gained the support of the Senate in opposing Antony, who by now was openly fighting Caesar's assassins. Though they clashed at the Battle of Mutina, Octavian and Antony quickly joined forces and unified the pro-Caesar faction against the Liberators. They also recruited Marcus Lepidus, creating the Second Triumvirate in November 43 BCE.

The Triumvirs decisively defeated the legions of Caesar's assassins at the Battle of Philippi in 42 BCE. Brutus and Cassius took their own lives rather than be captured. The three men then divided the Roman Republic between them. Antony took the eastern provinces (Greece, Asia Minor, and Syria), Octavian took the west, including Hispania and Gaul, and Lepidus received Africa. Egypt remained an independent client kingdom under Cleopatra VII, so it was outside Roman provincial administration, though Antony's close ties to Cleopatra gave him significant influence there. Antony and Cleopatra had a political and personal alliance, not a legal marriage, since Antony was married to Octavian's sister, Octavia.

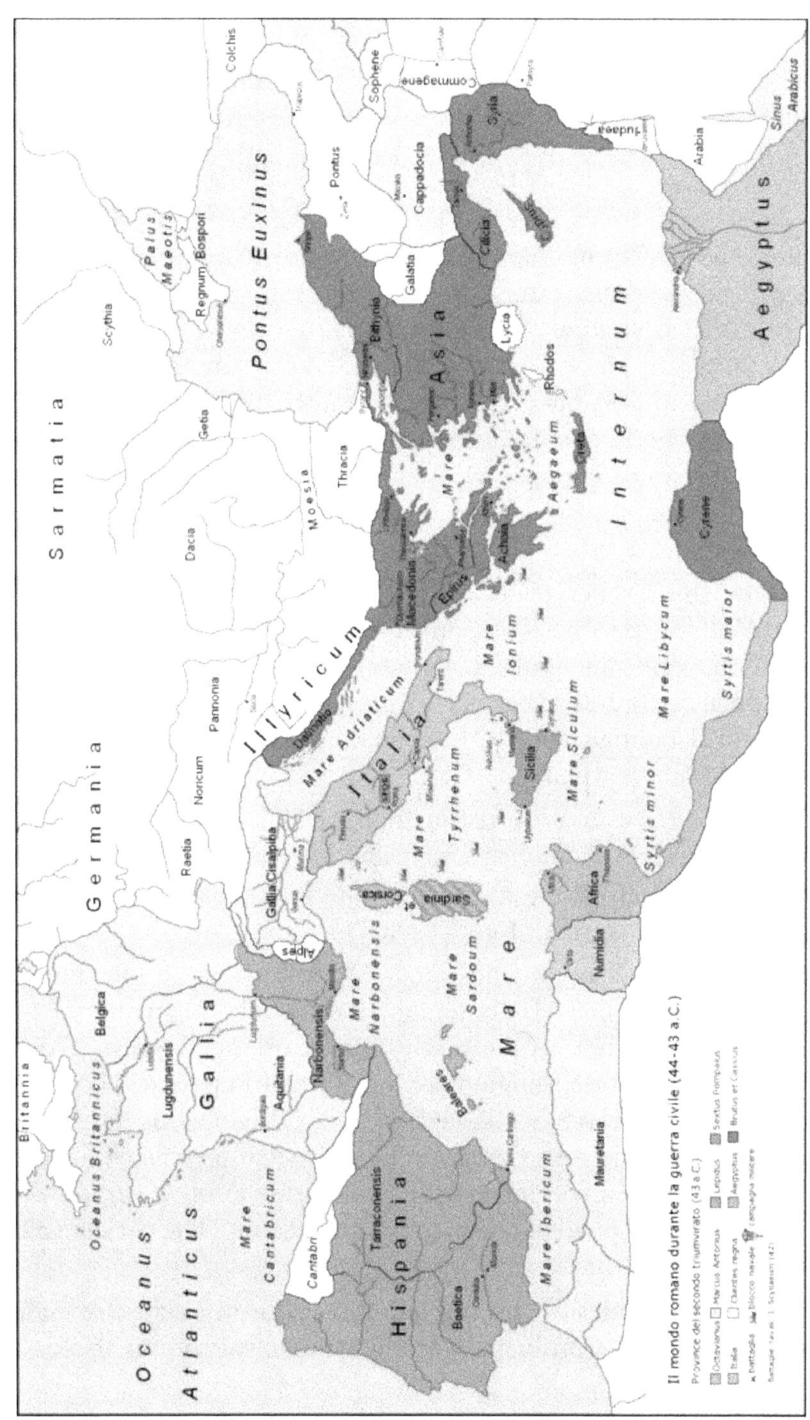

The Roman Empire during the Second Triumvirate[19]

The arrangement was unstable. Apart from the tension between Octavian and Antony, it took Octavian six years to subdue Sextus Pompey, who controlled Sicily and whose fleet threatened Rome's grain supply from Sicily and North Africa. The victory in this campaign was won not by Octavian but by his trusted commander, Marcus Vipsanius Agrippa. Agrippa was a general that any Roman emperor would want on his side. He was loyal, able, and prudent. So many times before, great generals had used their military reputations to reach for sole power. Agrippa could have done the same. He chose not to, though, remaining loyal to Octavian. He was rewarded abundantly. Among other things, he was allowed, and possibly even encouraged, to marry Octavian's daughter Julia. His career is a striking example of the power Roman generals wielded at this time. Agrippa was not simply a military officer. He built the original Pantheon, repaired Rome's aqueducts, and conducted one of the first comprehensive geographic surveys of the empire.

Antony, meanwhile, had barely survived a disastrous campaign in Parthia. With his own position consolidated, Octavian forced Lepidus out of the Triumvirate in 36 BCE. After this, Octavian claimed that "the whole of Italy swore its allegiance to him" and that he was positioned to lead the final confrontation.[i] He claimed allegiance from Gaul, Spain, Africa, Sicily, and Sardinia.

The war against Antony began in 31 BCE. At the naval Battle of Actium, Agrippa's fleet decisively defeated the combined forces of Antony and Cleopatra. Both fled to Egypt, and both took their own lives there the following year as Octavian's forces closed in.

With all political opponents gone, Octavian became the undisputed ruler of Rome, and in 27 BCE, he received the title of Augustus. Modern history remembers him as the first Roman emperor; however, Augustus preserved most of the institutions of the Roman Republic. Though these institutions were severely weakened and placed under his direct control, their preservation was necessary for him to avoid appearing tyrannical. His authority rested on a combination of powers, none of which individually meant autocracy but which together amounted to it. The Senate still met. Augustus just spoke first.

Almost two decades of civil war left the legions in a state that Augustus could not ignore. The problem wasn't just the military; it was also political.

[i] Octavianus Augustus, *Res Gestae divi Augusti*, p. 27

Armies in the late Roman Republic had been loyal to their commanders, not the state. Augustus intended to redirect that loyalty toward the princeps and the imperial institution itself.[i]

Marcus Claudius Marcellus, Augustus's nephew through his sister Octavia and later his son-in-law after marrying Augustus's daughter Julia, was gaining some following and could plausibly be positioned as a successor, which made the Senate nervous. Fears of a monarchical dynasty fed a conspiracy against Octavian in 23 BCE. That year proved to be a turning point. After surviving the conspiracy, Augustus fell seriously ill. Suetonius claims he came close to giving up entirely, but Augustus recovered and pushed through a significant restructuring of his own power. He gave up the consulship and instead consolidated authority through a combination of powers: tribunicia potestas, which gave him the rights of a tribune of the plebs, and imperium proconsulare maius, authority over the provincial armies, which meant he outranked any other commander. Combined with his status as princeps, these made him the dominant force in the state.

He was, formally, "first among equals." In practice, after 23 BCE, he had something very close to absolute power. The title imperator, which he had already used as part of his name, though it did not yet carry the meaning of "emperor" in any modern sense, became permanently attached to the office. Every ruler after him bore it. By controlling the army and representing the citizens, something later emperors would fail at spectacularly, Augustus paved the way for autocracy. Even though Rome was still formally a republic during his reign, Augustus had managed to achieve what Caesar and every ambitious general before him had not. He became, in every meaningful sense, the first Roman emperor.

Military reforms followed. First, he reduced the military from over fifty legions raised during the civil wars down to twenty-eight. The basic composition of a legion stayed largely the same. It comprised around five thousand heavy infantry who were armored and fought with the gladius and pilum. The legion was still organized into cohorts and centuries. What changed was the nature of the soldier himself. Augustus's legions were to be volunteer professionals, not mobilized citizens. These men would be better trained, serve longer terms, and receive better logistical support. Dedicated and expanded logistical support meant a Roman legion could sustain itself in the field for seasons while deep in enemy

---

[i] Princeps means "the first" or "most eminent."

territory, though seizing local supplies remained standard practice on a campaign regardless. Engineering capability was built in as well. Legionaries were expected to fight and also build fortifications, winter quarters, bridges, roads, and earthworks.

Twenty-eight legions could not cover everything. Other roles, including cavalry, scouts, archers, slingers, and border garrisons, needed to be filled, and this was where the auxilia came in. These were professional units recruited from non-citizens across the empire. Certain regions became associated with particular skills. For instance, the Balearic Islands were famous for their slingers, the best archers came from Crete and Syria, and Numidia was known for its light cavalry. Auxiliary units were roughly cohort-sized, ranging from five hundred to a thousand men depending on their role, which gave them both strategic and tactical flexibility. They could be attached to legions for major campaigns or spread across borders in peacetime. This smaller size also meant the foreign-composed auxilia would rarely, if ever, approach the numerical strength of the more politically reliable citizen legions nearby, even though at their peak, auxiliaries made up a substantial portion of the total Roman army. They were generally stationed outside their home regions, partly to prevent rebellion and partly to push assimilation into Roman military culture.

The need to protect the emperor personally and to maintain loyalty close to home was reflected in the founding of the Praetorian Guard. These men were recruited primarily from Italy, and they formed a distinct elite unit. Their role was to protect the emperor both on campaign and in Rome itself, where they were frequently the only military force present. Augustus had no major troubles with his Praetorian Guard. His successor, Tiberius, was considerably less fortunate. The Praetorians' close proximity to the emperor made them a political force in their own right, so they were effectively in a position to influence who lived and who didn't.

Augustus's reforms did not happen in a vacuum; they took place against the backdrop of almost continuous frontier warfare. Practically every year of his reign involved at least one significant military campaign, whether for conquest or suppressing a revolt. One of the early campaigns was the Cantabrian Wars (29–19 BCE). Augustus wanted to bring the last unconquered part of northern Hispania under Roman control. This wasn't a single war but a series of conflicts stretching across a decade. The difficulty wasn't the Romans' inability to fight; it was terrain and guerrilla tactics. The tribes of the region were skilled with light weapons, and the mountains made supply chains a constant problem. Augustus eventually committed eight legions, some thirty thousand soldiers, plus twenty thousand auxiliaries and naval support, to finish the job. Roman sources claim the Asturians preferred to die by their own hand rather than be taken prisoner. Death in arms was a form of victory in their opinion, and the Romans had little use for slaves who thought this way. Main resistance ended in 19 BCE, with smaller conflicts continuing until around 13 BCE.

Campaigns in northeastern Gaul (modern Belgium and the Netherlands) pushed the border to the Rhine, and fighting in the Balkans brought the frontier to the Danube. These two rivers would mark the limits of Roman power in Europe for centuries. Galatia, in what is now Turkey, was annexed in 25 BCE. Rebellions in Africa, Egypt, and Syria were pacified and settled.

As the empire expanded, new problems emerged. Tensions along the German frontier had been building, and by 12 BCE, the Germanic tribes near the mouth of the Rhine had been forced to acknowledge Roman authority. Augustus wanted more. He wanted a permanent Roman presence east of the Rhine. He gave the task to his stepson, Nero Claudius Drusus, who pushed Roman forces as far east as the Elbe by 9 BCE before dying that year after a riding accident. His brother, Tiberius, the future Roman emperor, took over and ran a successful campaign, though the province of Germania never really stabilized into anything resembling proper Roman provincial administration.

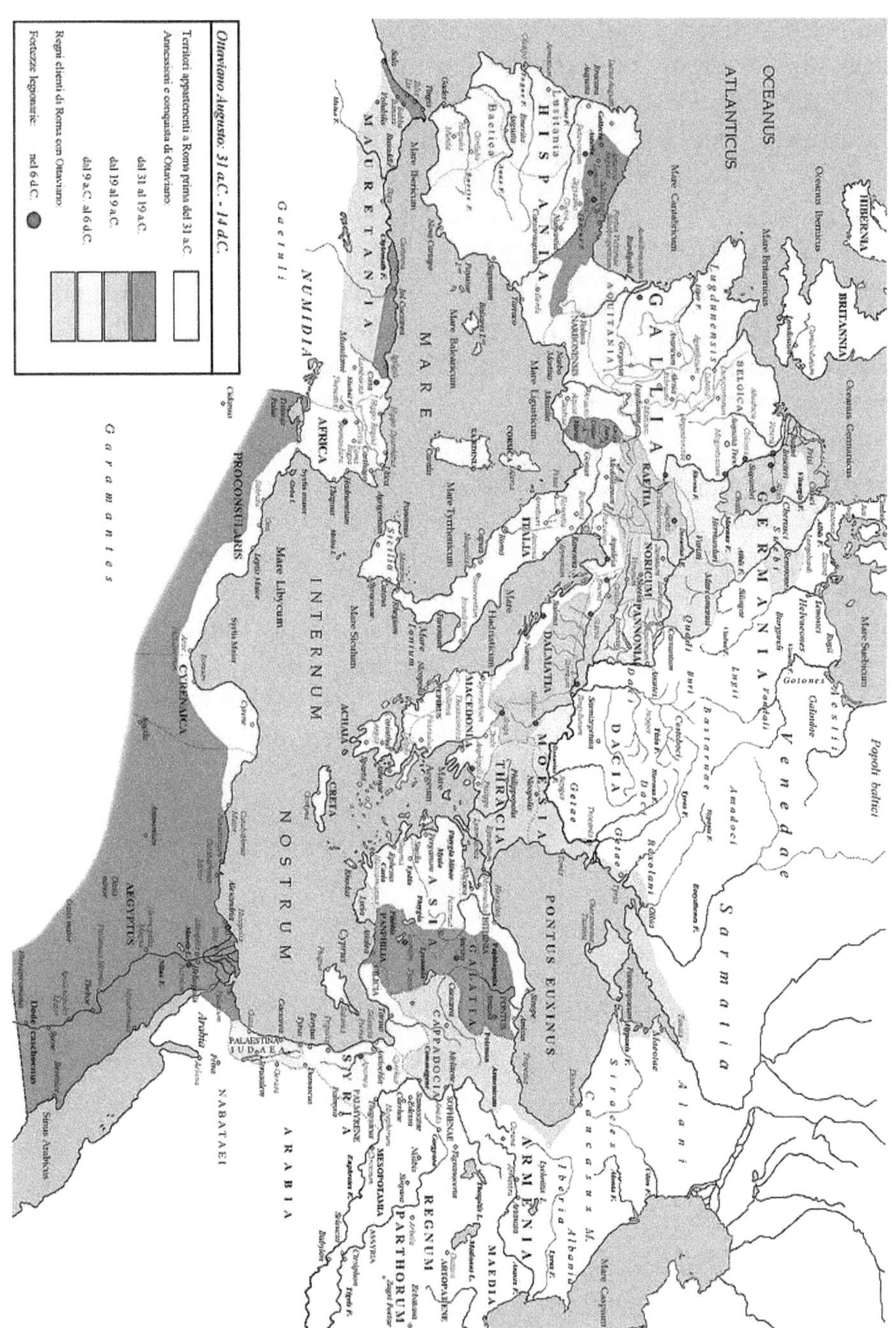

The Roman Empire under Augustus before the Pannonian revolt[20]

The plan after that was to push south into the territory of the Suebian kingdom under Maroboduus. Augustus began assembling a large army for a two-pronged attack. That plan collapsed when Pannonia erupted in revolt. The Illyrian tribes there were deeply unhappy with Roman taxation and military recruitment. Ancient sources put the rebel forces at around 200,000 infantry and 9,000 cavalry; although these figures are probably generous, the tribes still represented a serious threat.

Augustus reportedly told the Senate that if extreme measures were not taken immediately, the rebel army could reach Rome within days. Veterans were recalled to service. Slaves were freed and enlisted. Tiberius was put in command. Rather than seeking pitched battles, he controlled key positions and launched targeted strikes, grinding the revolt down over the years rather than breaking it in a single campaign. It worked, but it was slow and expensive.

The toll showed. The rebellion disrupted supply chains and triggered an economic crisis across the affected regions. Augustus's policies toward the newly conquered tribes were harsh, which deepened resentment rather than settling it. Even the equites, the wealthy citizen class that had generally supported Augustus, were unhappy. Dissatisfaction spread to the Senate and down to the plebs. The reputation Augustus had built over decades of stable, successful rule began to take a hit.

While Tiberius was still managing the Pannonian revolt, news came from Germany. Publius Quinctilius Varus, the governor charged with administering Roman territory east of the Rhine, had been ambushed and destroyed. Arminius, a chieftain of the Germanic Cherusci tribe who had been raised in Rome, trained in the Roman army, and held Roman citizenship, had spent years convincing Varus of his loyalty. One day, he led three Roman legions into the Teutoburg Forest and into a trap that had been carefully prepared. The legions were massacred. Varus killed himself. It was one of the worst military disasters in Roman history and the greatest humiliation of Augustus's reign. His reported response has become famous: "Quintili Vare, legiones redde!" ("Quintilius Varus, give me back my legions!").

Germanic warriors storming the field[21]

The disaster is sometimes framed as a consequence of Roman overreliance on foreign auxiliaries, but that explanation misses most of what actually happened. Poor intelligence, terrain that neutralized Roman tactical advantages, overconfidence, and Arminius's carefully maintained deception were the real causes. There had been similar episodes during Caesar's campaigns in Gaul, but the scale of the Teutoburg failure was unprecedented. The Roman army had not suffered a defeat this serious since Hannibal's victories in the Second Punic War.

Roman operations in Germany did not stop entirely after Teutoburg. Tiberius continued to campaign in the region, and after Augustus's death in 14 CE, Germanicus, son of the original Drusus, pushed further still under Tiberius's reign, with campaigns running into 16 CE. Augustus, however, had made his position clear before he died: the Rhine and Danube were where Roman expansion should stop. In the last years of his reign, he settled roughly half of all Roman legions along those two frontiers. That defensive posture in the West became the template for the emperors who came after him.

Earlier in his career, Augustus had been involved in Roman affairs in the East, namely Armenia, Syria, and Egypt, although he had dealings with Parthia and various client rulers. He directed policy and diplomacy there instead of personally campaigning. His attitude toward Eastern religions and cults was negative. Greek culture was treated differently, sitting just below Roman culture in the official hierarchy and receiving considerably more respect. Augustus revived old Roman religious customs and festivals, such as the Fratres Arvales and the Sodales Titii, and reformed the religious magistracies.

The reign of Augustus was as much a turning point in Roman history as it was a pivot of ancient history more broadly. His moderation and willingness to reward those close to him meant that there were no traitors in his inner circle. That was filled only with men he could trust to do their jobs. He was a man of broad enough view to understand that different situations called for different methods. He never abandoned Roman expansionism, but he knew when to stop, which was a skill the Roman Republic's generals had never quite developed. The institutional framework he built, the frontier decisions he made, and the foreign policy patterns he established all set the shape of the empire that followed him. The territory Rome controlled would grow larger in the centuries after him, but the pillars of how Rome would manage and defend that territory were put in place during his reign.

Chapter 7: Pax Romana: The Roman Army at Its Zenith

The period historians label the Pax Romana (the Roman Peace) is something of a misnomer. Rome frequently waged wars throughout this period in every corner of the empire. What the term actually refers to is internal peace and stability, especially when set against the intense civil unrest and military chaos that preceded and followed it. That internal order was maintained by the large professional armies of legions and auxilia manning Rome's borders and fighting its wars of conquest.

Augustus's campaigns had pushed the empire's frontiers to the Rhine and Danube. Further expansion into Germania was stopped decisively at the Battle of the Teutoburg Forest in 9 CE, where Arminius, a Germanic tribesman with Roman military training, destroyed three legions and their commander. Military activity in the region continued regardless, running until 16 CE, driven partly by the desire to avenge Teutoburg.

Augustus had reorganized the auxilia into a permanent corps of non-citizen soldiers around 27 BCE, building on auxiliary forces that had existed in the Roman Republic but formalizing and standardizing them for the first time. They were recruited mainly from the *peregrini*, free provincial subjects without Roman citizenship, as well as from peoples beyond the empire's borders whom Romans collectively termed "barbarians," a word derived from the Greek for "foreigner." The term basically meant someone outside of the Roman civilization, though it often carried the sense of being uncivilized. These non-citizen soldiers were regularly stationed in provinces other than where they had been raised, partly to encourage Romanization and partly to reduce the risk of local loyalties overriding military loyalties. The names of auxiliary units persisted long after the original recruits were gone, and by the later empire, auxiliary soldiers were often comparable to legionaries in training and capability, though their equipment and roles sometimes differed.

The most prominent Roman commander of this period was Germanicus Julius Caesar. He was not a descendant of Julius Caesar, but he carried the name as part of the imperial family naming system that Augustus's adoption had set in motion. He was the nephew and adopted son of Emperor Tiberius. Germanicus defeated Germanic forces in several engagements, including the Battles of Idistaviso and the Angrivarian Wall, and recovered two of the three legionary aquilae (the eagle standards) lost in the forests of Teutoburg. These were real military achievements, though they did not result in permanent Roman control of Germania east of the Rhine. It was because of these campaigns that he received the agnomen Germanicus. He died in Syria in 19 CE.

Germania beyond the Rhine remained unconquered, aside from the fertile plains of the Lower Rhine and the strip of territory between the Rhine and Danube. The reasons were straightforward enough. Central Europe was far more heavily forested than it is today, the population was hostile, the region offered little material wealth compared to other areas, and there were no natural defensible borders to anchor a frontier. Holding the Limes Germanicus, the Germanic frontier, would remain one of the Roman army's longest and most difficult commitments for the rest of the empire's existence.

Roman auxiliary infantry crossing a river, probably the Danube[22]

The next major campaign was the conquest of Britain, beginning in 43 CE under Emperor Claudius. It lasted over forty years in its main phase, although Roman campaigns in Britain persisted for decades after the initial conquest. Although Hadrian's Wall was built in the early 2nd century CE to stabilize the northern frontier, fighting in northern Britain went on well beyond it.

Rome's eastern border with Parthia was also under a lot of pressure, with wars running from 59 to 64 CE and continuing throughout the 1st century. Revolts added to the strain. The Great Jewish Revolt brought widespread destruction to the province of Judaea from 66 to 74 CE. Near the Rhine Delta, the Batavi tribe rose in 70 CE and destroyed two full legions before a large Roman force finally suppressed them. In Britain, Iceni Queen Boudica staged a revolt that came closer to succeeding than Rome would have liked to admit. These uprisings had different causes and contexts. Many stemmed from local political and economic grievances that had been building for years, though some were also shaped by the instability running through the empire during this period, particularly the civil wars of 69 CE.

That year, known in Roman history as the Year of the Four Emperors, was the first major imperial civil war involving multiple rival claimants to the throne since the time of Augustus. It was brief, but it showed that the principate was not as settled as it had appeared and that the army remained the ultimate arbiter of power. Vespasian, who prevailed, had the broadest military backing of any of the claimants, built in large part on his own record and his son Titus's conduct during the Jewish Revolt. He founded the Flavian dynasty, which replaced the Julio-Claudians. He ended five generations of stepsons, nephews, and adopted heirs who had ruled from Augustus until Nero.

The empire reached its greatest geographical extent under Trajan (r. 98–117), whose Dacian campaigns and later push into Mesopotamia extended Roman rule as far as the Persian Gulf. Augustus had believed that victory was the precondition for peace. His own formulation of it, recorded in the *Res Gestae*, described a peace won through conquest: "Per totum imperium populi Romani terra marique ... parta victoriis pax" ("Throughout the whole Roman Empire, on land and sea, a peace won by victories"). The coins of the period bore the inscription Pax Augusti, "Augustus's peace." It was not a peace achieved by standing still.

A Roman coin from 243–244 stating "Pax Augusti" on the reverse[23]

The Pax Romana represents the peak of Roman military capability, though that phrase needs unpacking. Military capability is not simply a matter of how well individual soldiers fight or what armor they wear. The lorica segmentata, the segmented metal armor most associated with the Roman soldier of this period, was not objectively superior to everything it faced. For instance, Roman soldiers in the Dacian Wars suffered serious wounds from the falx, a two-handed Dacian bladed weapon capable of getting under or around conventional armor. Even at the height of Roman dominance, defeat was not unknown.

A recreation of the lorica segmentata[24]

What made the imperial Roman army of the Pax Romana exceptional was its ability to operate across the full extent of the empire, sometimes on multiple frontiers at the same time, in practically any climate or season, and to sustain itself in hostile territory for extended periods, often years. That kind of capability depended on a set of disciplines that went well beyond individual fighting skills. Logistics—producing or foraging and then moving adequate supplies—was foundational. Intelligence gathering, military engineering, the ability to construct roads, bridges, fortifications, and siege equipment in the field all contributed to what made a Roman army effective rather than just large.

On the broader scale, the empire had to maintain a manpower pool large enough to fill professional armies and a farming base capable of feeding them in peacetime. It needed an economy stable enough to pay regular salaries and equip hundreds of thousands of soldiers continuously. Estimates suggest that somewhere between 50 and 70 percent of the imperial budget went to the military. It was the dominant expense of the Roman state for the remainder of its existence, and everything else was built around it.

Behind just one legion of some five thousand fighting men stood a vast support structure. There were non-combat personnel, mules, horses, wagons, attendant slaves, camp followers, sutlers (merchants who followed armies to sell goods), cooks, and craftsmen. At full strength, around five hundred soldiers in a legion, roughly 10 percent, were immunes, or dedicated specialists excused from some routine duties and paid better for it. These men were still trained legionaries, so they were capable of fighting when needed. They included engineers, artillerymen, drill instructors, carpenters, medics, and surveyors.

This professional core meant that a Roman army in the field during the principate was, in both peace and war, effectively a traveling construction crew. On campaign, the army built roads as it advanced, allowing for reinforcements, resupply, and retreat. Roman road-building was good enough that some roads survive today. Many modern European routes follow the general alignments of roads the Romans laid down two thousand years ago.

Military construction went well beyond roads. Over three hundred fortresses were erected along the Rhine and Danube alone, plus countless castra (forts and legionary quarters), many of which grew into cities over the centuries. London, Cologne, and Belgrade started as Roman military installations. The Romans also perfected the large-scale construction of durable load-bearing bridges, particularly stone arch bridges, building them in permanent stone, in wood, and as pontoon crossings. Many stone bridges survive today; some are still even used. Others are known only through records, such as Caesar's two wooden bridges across the Rhine and Trajan's bridge across the Danube, the longest bridge in antiquity at over a kilometer in length.

During the nearly two centuries of the Pax Romana, the Roman army, as it had done before and would continue to do afterward, adapted constantly, taking on new roles, developing new tactics, and finding ways to counter what enemies threw at it. This period saw the full development of the Roman legionary as heavy armored infantry. They used the gladius, scutum, and pila. They fought in tight formations where soldiers supported one another and exhausted front-line troops could be rotated to the rear and replaced with fresher men. Against the most common infantry opponent of the period—a non-professional fighter with a spear and shield—a disciplined Roman formation in open ground had a decisive advantage. The original manipular system had been developed, after all, to counter the Greek phalanx.

The problem was that the battles the Romans wanted to fight were relatively uncommon. Many of Rome's enemies understood Roman tactics well enough to avoid pitched battle when possible, which meant the Romans often had to fight on worse terms, with exposed flanks or on difficult terrain, or take what they wanted through siege. Roman soldiers became capable of constructing elaborate siegeworks and manufacturing a range of siege weapons, like the *scorpio* and ballista for medium-range fire and, later, the onager for heavier bombardment. They also used scaling ladders, siege towers, and battering rams.

The Romans learned from disasters. The Battle of Carrhae in 53 BCE, where Crassus's legions were destroyed by Parthian cavalry, highlighted the Romans' vulnerability to mobile horse-mounted armies. The fast-moving horse archers and heavily armored cataphracts were the enemies that Rome kept encountering on the eastern frontier. Legionaries already had anti-cavalry responses, such as the square formation and using pila as spears to extend their reach against riders, but Carrhae sharpened the emphasis on discipline when facing mounted attacks. It also pushed the Roman cavalry, which was largely drawn from foreign auxilia, toward greater tactical standardization. They would begin to regularly harass enemy cavalry, protect friendly infantry, and keep the flanks clear. In Britain, chariot-mounted archers and javelin throwers posed a different kind of problem, and Roman tactics adjusted there too.

The Teutoburg disaster led to improvements in scouting. Roman armies in the field operated with several layers of intelligence-gathering. Exploratores worked ahead of the column, reconnoitering the ground. Speculatores ranged farther still, operating well ahead of the army and sometimes behind enemy lines; they were intelligence agents as much as scouts. The procursatores covered the army's immediate surroundings. Together, they gave Roman commanders a picture of enemy positions, movements, and strength that most opponents simply couldn't match. That intelligence advantage translated directly into initiative.

None of it would have worked without discipline. Josephus, who watched the Roman army train, wrote that their drills were no different from the real thing. He called them bloodless battles, while their actual battles were bloody drills.[i] The first thing a recruit learned was the military pace and his place in formation. Training began with wooden weapons and then progressed to mock battles. Cavalry developed a complex sequence of drills known as the hippika gymnasia. Roman training emphasized both individual skill and coordinated unit performance to an unusual degree. Most enemies had experienced warriors, but the Romans had something those warriors generally did not: the ability to function as a unit under pressure.

In actual combat, casualties during the main phase of close engagement were relatively light on both sides since each side's soldiers were protecting and being protected by those next to them. Wounded men could be pulled back. The real danger was a flank or rear attack, which threatened not just physical vulnerability but psychological cohesion. Enough disruption would lead to panic, panic would lead to a rout, and a routed army would break apart and be slaughtered piecemeal. Roman discipline reduced the likelihood of routs, though they did occasionally occur. Professional soldiers accustomed to combat conditions were simply less likely to break, and if they were losing, they often kept fighting rather than running. Even during construction work, this discipline held. Legionaries building a fortified camp were expected to be able to drop their tools and repel an attack.

The Roman army fought, almost as a rule, to keep the initiative. They were to stay on the offensive and force the enemy to respond. When the empire's later history forced Rome into an increasing number of defensive wars, the legionary system of the Pax Romana found itself poorly adapted to the new situation. Holding a static frontier was not what it had been built for.

The end of the Roman Peace came from several directions at once. The Antonine Plague, which lasted from 165 to 180 CE, tore through the

---

[i] Josephus, Flavius, *Wars of the Jews.*

empire's population and disrupted the manpower available to the legions. The economic consequences were severe. Emperor Marcus Aurelius responded by devaluing the currency, reducing the silver content of the denarius, which generated short-term revenue at the cost of longer-term stability. Plus, the currency had already been debased multiple times before. He did it to pay the army. Everything else in the economy suffered for it, though, and the inflation that followed made the underlying instability worse. The Marcomannic Wars on the Upper Danube dominated Marcus Aurelius's reign, and before that, his co-emperor, Lucius Verus, had fought an expensive war against Parthia. Both were won, but both drained resources that Rome could not easily replace.

Marcus Aurelius was succeeded by his son Commodus, who made things worse rather than better. He was assassinated in 193, the Year of the Five Emperors. Roman legionaries once again clashed against each other in civil war, and a series of assassinations and armed conflicts shook the empire's political structure. The crisis was eventually contained under Septimius Severus, the last man standing from that year's succession struggle. However, the long-term consequences for the army were significant.

The distinction between citizen legionaries and non-citizen auxilia was gradually eroded after the Constitutio Antoniniana, also known as the Edict of Caracalla, of 212. Septimius's successor, Caracalla, extended full Roman citizenship to every free man in the empire. The reasons behind it are still debated. He could have been expanding the tax base since full citizens paid more, broadening the manpower pool for the legions, or building personal loyalty to the man who had granted citizenship. It was probably some combination of all three.

In 216, Caracalla launched a campaign against Parthia. He was assassinated within the year. His successor, Macrinus, lasted less than a year. He was overthrown without ever visiting Rome to be confirmed by the Senate, and his attempts to stabilize the economy at the army's expense predictably ended in military revolt. Elagabalus, who followed, did little to reverse the decline. His successor, Severus Alexander (r. 222-235), made real progress in stabilizing the empire's fortunes, but when he was assassinated in 235, Rome entered the Crisis of the Third Century, a period of near-continuous civil war and external pressure that transformed the empire almost beyond recognition.

The concept of the Pax Romana outlasted Rome itself. Later empires, Byzantine and in the Christian West, looked back on the period as a model worth imitating, even if they never quite managed to reproduce it.

Chapter 8: Decline and Fall: Military Challenges in Late Antiquity

The peace did not collapse overnight, but the death of Marcus Aurelius in 180 CE is generally taken as the symbolic end of the Pax Romana. What followed was a period of political, military, and economic crisis for the empire and for the army that held it together.

Aurelius was succeeded by his son Commodus, who was an ineffective and self-indulgent ruler. The contrast with the so-called Five Good Emperors was stark.[i] Those men had come to power through adoption and selection on merit, or something close to it. Later emperors came through coups, bribery, and assassination.

Lucius Septimius Severus was a product of that new reality. He gained power through the army, and the army remained the foundation of everything he did. Cassius Dio attributes these words to him: "Get along, pay the soldiers substantially, and don't worry about the rest."[ii] He fought a long civil war to secure his position and pushed through significant reforms once he had it. For instance, he dismissed the existing Praetorian Guard and replaced it with soldiers personally loyal to him. He also campaigned against the Parthians. He died in 211 during a campaign against the Caledonians in Britain.

---

[i] The Five Good Emperors were Nerva, Trajan, Hadrian, Antoninus Pius, and Marcus Aurelius.

[ii] Mashkin, Nikolai, *A History of Ancient Rome,* Gospolitizdat, 1956, p. 363

Severus was succeeded by his two sons, Marcus Aurelius Antoninus, known to history as Caracalla, and Publius Septimius Geta. Both were recognized as co-rulers, but Caracalla quickly emerged as the dominant one. He had Geta murdered not long after, becoming the sole ruler. He spent money the empire didn't have trying to buy off enemies and secure loyalty, but it wasn't enough. In 217, he was assassinated as part of a conspiracy organized by the Praetorian Prefect Macrinus.

Political instability after that became something close to the norm. The mid-3rd century crisis, running roughly from 235 to 284, saw more than twenty emperors and numerous usurpers rule in the space of fifty years. Most of them died violently. They were frequently killed by the same soldiers who had elevated them. Civil war was almost continuous. Financial pressure made everything else worse.

The military consequences were severe. Germanic raiders pushed deep into the western provinces. The East was overrun in large parts by the Sassanid Persians, who had replaced the Parthians as Rome's main eastern rival and were considerably more aggressive. In 251, Emperor Decius was killed when his army was defeated by the Goths; it was the first time a reigning Roman emperor had died in battle against a foreign enemy. In 260, Valerian was captured by the Persians. Two breakaway states emerged during this period: a short-lived Gallic Empire in the west and the Palmyrene Empire in the east, centered on the Kingdom of Palmyra, both of which temporarily held large chunks of what had been Roman territory. Meanwhile, civil wars kept draining the army's capacity to deal with any of it.

Valerian's son Gallienus, already a joint ruler since 253, succeeded him. His reign was defined by one crisis after another, and he was killed in 268 during one of the many uprisings against him. The soldiers chose Claudius II as his replacement. He moved quickly. His first major engagement was against the Alamanni, who had pushed into Italy. He defeated them at the Battle of Lake Benacus in 268, earning the title Germanicus Maximus for it. Then he turned east to deal with the Goths in the Balkans.

He found their army at Naissus, in what is now Serbia, in 269. The battle was hard and bloody. The Romans broke the Gothic force partly through a feigned retreat, drawing them out of position before hitting them from prepared positions. The future emperor Aurelian apparently played an important role in the final stages of the fighting, though the victory belonged to Claudius as much as anyone. Tens of thousands of Goths were killed or captured. It was the kind of decisive result the empire badly needed. However, the rest of the empire was still burning, and Claudius did not live long enough to deal with it; he died shortly after Naissus, probably of plague. His brother Quintillus took the throne and lasted only weeks before the legions around Sirmium declared for someone else entirely.

That someone was Aurelian, later called the Restitutor Orbis ("Restorer of the World"). He was a barracks emperor, which means the legions proclaimed him emperor. The loyalty of his soldiers brought him to power rather than his birth or senatorial backing. His father had worked as a tenant farmer for a senator in the Roman province of Pannonia in the Balkans, which was not exactly the traditional background for an emperor. Earlier emperors had typically come from the senatorial aristocracy, while the 3rd century increasingly produced emperors who had risen entirely through their military careers. Aurelian was the fullest expression of that pattern.

That pattern itself is worth pausing on because it represents one of the most significant structural shifts of the entire period. The great commanders of earlier centuries—Marius, Sulla, Pompey, Antony, Caesar, Augustus, and Germanicus—had all been tied to the highest aristocratic networks from birth. Military talent and aristocratic connections went together. Vespasian had been an early crack in that pattern. He was not from the old elite and had to fight his way to the throne through the chaos of 69 CE. The military became the primary route to imperial power. Anyone with enough soldiers and enough ability to hold their loyalty could try for it, and many did.

The consequences of this ran deep. As rivals for the throne spent more time with provincial armies, those armies started behaving more like personal retinues. The composition of senior officer ranks shifted. Senatorial representation declined steadily through the 3rd century, replaced by equestrian career soldiers who had spent their lives in the army and held no civil offices. These were the men most likely to plot against sitting emperors and put forward candidates from their own circles. Emperors spent so much time on campaigns that they became increasingly distant from Rome and Roman political life. The court moved with the army. To become emperor, one needed popularity with the troops and the ability to lead them in battle. That was more or less it. And because that was the qualification, no emperor could safely hand command of a major army to a potential rival, unlike the old consular system, where military command was transferred on a fixed schedule, whether anyone liked it or not. The result was paranoia, fragmentation, and a cycle of rebellion that fed on itself.

Aurelian saw all of this clearly and somehow managed to cut through it. He reunited the empire, reconquering the Palmyrene territories in the east and suppressing the Gallic breakaway state in the west, and held it together through a combination of military force and political reform. He elevated the cult of Sol Invictus, the Unconquered Sun, building a major temple in Rome and promoting it. The cult had existed before his reign, but Aurelian gave it unprecedented prominence within the imperial religious system. The symbolism was clear. A single sun ruling the heavens could serve as a powerful metaphor for a restored and unified empire.

He also turned to the food supply. Rome had a long tradition of subsidized grain distribution for the poorest citizens, dating back to the Roman Republic, but Aurelian expanded it significantly, switching from raw grain to baked bread and, in some cases, adding other commodities such as oil, pork, and salt. Keeping the urban poor fed was both a genuine welfare measure and a practical political calculation, and Aurelian was clear-eyed enough to pursue both at once. It earned him real popularity in the city.

He knew there would be more usurpers. There always were. He spent his reign moving between suppressing rebellions and implementing reforms, never fully separating the two problems because they could not really be separated. The crisis that had consumed the 3rd century was not solved by any single campaign or any single reform. What Aurelian did was stabilize enough of it to give the empire a foundation to build on, which is why the title Restitutor Orbis stuck.

After several decades of crisis, a measure of stability returned under Diocletian. He held off foreign invaders, and the reforms he pushed through, some of which were already in motion under his predecessors, addressed both the political and military foundations of the empire. His most significant innovation was the Tetrarchy, a system of divided imperial power with two senior emperors, each titled Augustus, ruling the Eastern and Western halves respectively. They would be supported by a junior colleague called Caesar. The idea was practical on two levels. There would be enough commanders to handle simultaneous crises across a vast empire and a built-in succession system that gave ambitious men with armies a legitimate path forward rather than a reason to rebel. Diocletian managed to reduce, at least for a time, the constant threat of assassination and forced abdication that had defined the previous half-century. Elite court units, such as the *protectores domestici*, developed during this period. The Praetorian Guard continued to exist until it was abolished by Constantine in 312.

Diocletian and Maximian on an aureus (gold coin)[25]

The system held while Diocletian was in control. Almost as soon as he and his Western colleague Maximian retired in 305, it began to fracture. A long series of civil wars followed. The conflict was eventually settled when Constantine defeated his last rival in 324 and ruled as sole emperor until his death in 337.

Afterward, however, the divided imperial rule reasserted itself. Constantine preserved the administrative system developed under Diocletian but strengthened the authority of the praetorian prefects, transforming them into senior civilian officials. Over the course of the 4th century, this structure developed into the four great praetorian prefectures of the East, Illyricum, Italy, and Gaul.

The army itself had been changing throughout this period. The *comitatenses* emerged as mobile field armies drawn from soldiers across the empire. They were capable of rapid deployment to a crisis. Provincial armies were reorganized into frontier garrisons known as *limitanei*. They were recruited largely from local populations within the empire and tasked with holding the borders rather than fighting major campaigns. Lactantius, an early Christian writer, claims the total number of soldiers quadrupled under Diocletian, but this is almost certainly an exaggeration. The overall number did increase, but individual unit sizes shrank. More than sixty legions appear to have existed by the end of the 3rd century, but at around a thousand men each rather than the five thousand of the early empire. Cavalry units called *vexillationes* and the older alae and infantry cohorts mustered around five to six hundred men apiece.

Equipment changed too. The rectangular scutum and heavy pilum, the defining equipment of the earlier legionaries, became less common through the 3rd century, replaced by oval shields and lighter spears, such as the lancea. Some units carried lead-weighted darts called plumbatae, slotted into hollows in their shields, up to five per man. Most soldiers wore scale or mail armor and iron helmets. Ammianus, a Roman historian, records Roman infantry raising the *baritus* before battle. This was a Germanic war cry that grew steadily in volume and was used to build courage before an engagement. The adoption of a Germanic battle practice by a Roman army is itself a comment on how much the relationship between Rome and its neighbors had changed.

Tactics varied by theater. Against the Persians in the East, heavily armored cavalry units, the cataphracts and clibanarii, became more prominent in response to the Persian heavy cavalry. Persian archers made advancing at pace more effective than standing to receive the attack, so Eastern engagements more often saw Romans closing quickly rather than holding their ground. In the West, where the main threat was barbarian infantry charges, the opposite approach applied. They were to hold the line in good order, absorb the charge, and then respond from a position of stability.

Through the 4th and 5th centuries, the empire's reliance on foederati, non-Roman tribal groups serving under a treaty, grew steadily. These were different from the traditional auxiliaries. Foederati maintained their own leadership structures, identities, and ways of fighting. They were granted land in exchange for military service, but they were not integrated into the Roman command structure in the same way. They filled gaps that the empire could no longer fill with its own manpower, but in the long term, they were harder to control. Their tribal loyalties took precedence over Roman ones when the two came into conflict.

The crisis point came in 376 CE. A large group of Goths, under pressure from the Huns moving in from the east, asked permission to cross the Danube and settle within the empire. Emperor Valens allowed it. What followed was a catastrophe of Roman administration rather than Gothic aggression. Roman officials exploited and abused the settlers, creating the conditions for revolt.

The resulting conflict ended at the Battle of Adrianople in 378. The size of both armies is uncertain and debated, but the outcome was not. The Romans were destroyed. Emperor Valens probably died on the field, though his body was never recovered; most of his guards had abandoned him during the collapse. Many prominent commanders died alongside him. Survivors escaped during the night. Later writers, including Tyrannius Rufinus, described the battle as the beginning of the empire's troubles, and in retrospect, it is hard to argue with that assessment. It was not that the army was fundamentally broken—it still remained a professional force with real capability—but the defeat forced the empire to depend more on foederati since the losses at Adrianople could not easily be replaced from Roman sources.

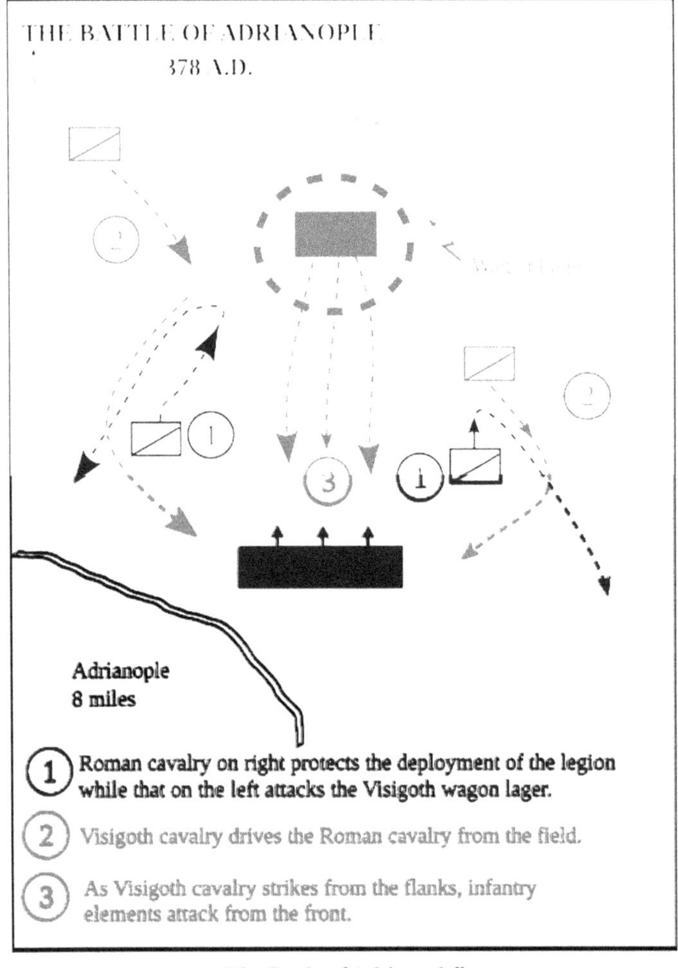

The Battle of Adrianople[26]

By 382, the Goths had accepted peace terms and agreed to provide troops for Rome. The defeat had been severe, but the Roman Empire was still standing. Few people at the time imagined it might actually fall.

One of those Gothic foederati commanders was Alaric. He rose to become king of the Visigoths and spent years seeking formal recognition and land grants from the Western imperial government. Emperor Honorius, ruling from the relative safety of Ravenna, refused to deal with him seriously. Alaric responded by besieging Rome.

The Roman Senate sent envoys to negotiate terms. Alaric's demands were gold, silver, luxury goods, and the release of barbarian slaves. When one envoy asked what would be left for the citizens of Rome, Alaric answered, "Their lives."[i] Rome paid and released the slaves, who promptly joined Alaric's force, making it larger. A second siege followed. A failed attempt by Emperor Honorius to ambush Alaric during negotiations was the end of diplomacy between the two sides. Alaric besieged Rome a third time, and in 410, his forces entered through the Salarian Gate, which had likely been opened by slaves or sympathizers from within.

The sack lasted three days. Looting was extensive, but the violence was restrained by the standards of ancient warfare. There was no mass killing of civilians, and most buildings were left standing. Churches, including St. Peter's Basilica, were left untouched. However, the symbolic damage was enormous. Rome had not been sacked in eight hundred years. The Eternal City, the center of the Roman world, had proven to be neither eternal nor invincible.

Nobles were taken captive, among them the emperor's sister, Galla Placidia. Refugees scattered to Africa, Egypt, and the Eastern provinces. After three days, Alaric left, moving south through Campania, Lucania, and Calabria. He intended to eventually cross to Sicily and Africa. He never got there. He died within months of the sack and was buried, according to legend, with his treasure.

---

[i] Zosimus, *New History*, 2017.

The sack of Rome in 410 by the barbarians[27]

The Visigoths settled in southwestern Gaul in 418 and would later fight alongside Rome against a common enemy from the East. However, the pattern was already clear. Roman victories were becoming rarer and less decisive. The empire was conceding ground it could not recover.

Several barbarian groups, such as the Vandals, Suebi, and Alans, among others, had entered Hispania in 409. The Vandals consolidated control of parts of the peninsula by 420 and then crossed to Africa in 429, seizing large parts of Numidia. In the 430s, Attila unified the Huns and began pushing into the Pannonian and Moesian provinces.

Relations between the Western Roman Empire and the Huns remained workable until around 450. In 451, Attila crossed the Rhine with a large coalition of allied tribes and drove into Gaul. The Western Roman general Flavius Aetius, called "the last of the Romans" by contemporaries, put together a response that was itself a symptom of how much had changed. He assembled an alliance of Romans, Visigoths under Theodoric I, Franks, and Alans. He then met Attila at the Catalaunian Plains.[i]

The fighting was savage, with heavy cavalry charges and close infantry combat. Casualties were enormous. Tens of thousands died, at the very least. Theodoric was killed. His son Thorismund took command of the Visigoths and wanted to press the assault on Attila's camp. Aetius talked him out of it, sending him home to secure the Visigoth throne while applying enough pressure on Attila to force a retreat. It was a calculated decision. The Romans and their allies defeated the Huns enough to stop their advance without destroying them so completely that the balance of power in the region collapsed in unpredictable ways.

Attila retreated, but he was not finished. He turned to Italy, where he continued raiding until 453. He died that year, reportedly on his wedding night. The coalition that had stopped him dissolved almost immediately after. It had been a temporary alignment of interests, not a long-lasting alliance.

Aetius did not survive long either. His political rivalry with Emperor Valentinian III ended with his assassination. After his death, the Western Roman Empire moved faster toward collapse. The Vandal king Gaiseric raided Rome in 455; this was a more systematic plundering than Alaric's sack forty-five years earlier. Between 470 and 490, the Goths absorbed the remaining western provinces in Gaul. In 476, the Germanic commander Odoacer deposed Romulus Augustulus, the last Western Roman emperor, a teenager whose very name combined the founder of Rome with the founder of the empire. Odoacer sent the imperial insignia to Constantinople. The Western Roman Empire was over.

What followed was not a clean break. The Eastern Roman Empire continued, doing so for another thousand years. The new kingdoms that replaced Rome in the West were built on Roman administrative frameworks, Roman law, and Roman Christianity. The army that had

[i] Mesihović, Salmedin, *Orbis Romanvs,* University of Sarajevo, 2015, p. 2407

conquered most of the known world left behind something more lasting than the institution itself: a model of organized military power, logistical capability, and disciplined force that shaped European warfare for centuries. The Eastern Roman Empire, Byzantium, carried that inheritance forward, adapting it through a millennium of its own wars and crises. But even in the West, where the legions were gone, the Romans were never entirely gone.

Conclusion

Roman military history is a record of battles, generals, and tactics, but also of a civilization's capacity to adapt and endure. The legions were among the most effective military units of the ancient world, having risen from modest origins to dominance over large parts of Europe, North Africa, and the Near East.

That story has never really left the popular imagination. The French film series *Asterix and Obelix* brought Roman legions, their standards, and their fortified camps to generations of viewers. *Gladiator* gave audiences a Roman general destroyed by the whimsical cruelty of Commodus and thrown into the arena. The TV series *Rome* traced the violent transition from the Roman Republic to the Roman Empire with unusual attention to the military conflicts that drove it. The Romans are everywhere in popular culture and have been for a long time.

It is hard to overstate how central military affairs were to Rome's development from the very beginning. The founding myth itself is a military story. Aeneas, a Trojan warrior, flees the fall of Troy and makes his way to Italy, where his descendants eventually produce Romulus and Remus, who founded the city of Rome. The start of Roman history and the start of Roman military history are pretty much the same moment. What followed across the next twelve centuries shaped the world in ways still visible today. Discipline, training, well-made equipment, and organized logistical support were the practical foundations of Roman military success. However, underlying all of it was flexibility. The same basic structure could be adapted to fight different enemies across radically different terrain, from the forests of Germania to the deserts of North Africa to the hills of Judaea.

That system did not emerge fully formed. Roman warfare began by absorbing Etruscan and Greek practices, adapting the phalanx, and then moving beyond it as the demands of Italian and then Mediterranean conquest required something more versatile. The reforms associated with Gaius Marius accelerated the transition toward a more professional army. He standardized equipment, opened the legions to volunteers regardless of property, and deepened the bond between soldiers and their commanders. That bond had consequences, as the civil wars of the late Roman Republic demonstrated. However, it also produced an army with extraordinary cohesion and endurance. The legions created a model of military organization that outlasted the empire that built them.

Roman military traditions fed into the Byzantine system and moved through Byzantium and other channels into the broader military cultures of medieval Europe. Napoleon Bonaparte consciously adopted Roman symbolism, such as eagle standards for his regiments, the name velites for light infantry units in his guard, and cavalry helmets modeled on Roman designs. The Prussians and Russians put eagles on their flags, and the titles their rulers bore (Kaiser and Tsar) were both derived from Caesar. George S. Patton, one of the most prominent American generals of the Second World War and a serious student of Roman military history, believed he had been a Roman legionary in a previous life. He claimed to remember it while campaigning in Sicily in 1943, retracing ground where Roman armies had fought more than two thousand years before. The term legion itself survives in modern military usage. The French Foreign Legion carries the name, though the connection is symbolic rather than institutional.

Roman road-building and logistical organization set patterns that shaped how later armies thought about supply and movement. The study of Roman campaigns, both their victories and their catastrophic defeats, remains part of military education today. The disasters are analyzed as carefully as the triumphs because the Roman army's failures are as instructive as its successes.

The Roman Empire fell. The causes were multiple and interconnected. There was sustained external pressure, chronic internal political instability, and socio-economic strains that neither discipline nor tactical ingenuity could fully compensate for. However, the military system Rome built proved more durable than the state it served. Its ideas, its organizational logic, its terminology, and its examples passed into the traditions of the armies that came after it, and they are still being studied, argued over, and in some cases imitated today.

Part 2: Julius Caesar

An Enthralling Guide to the Conquest, Power, and Assassination of Rome's Eternal Dictator

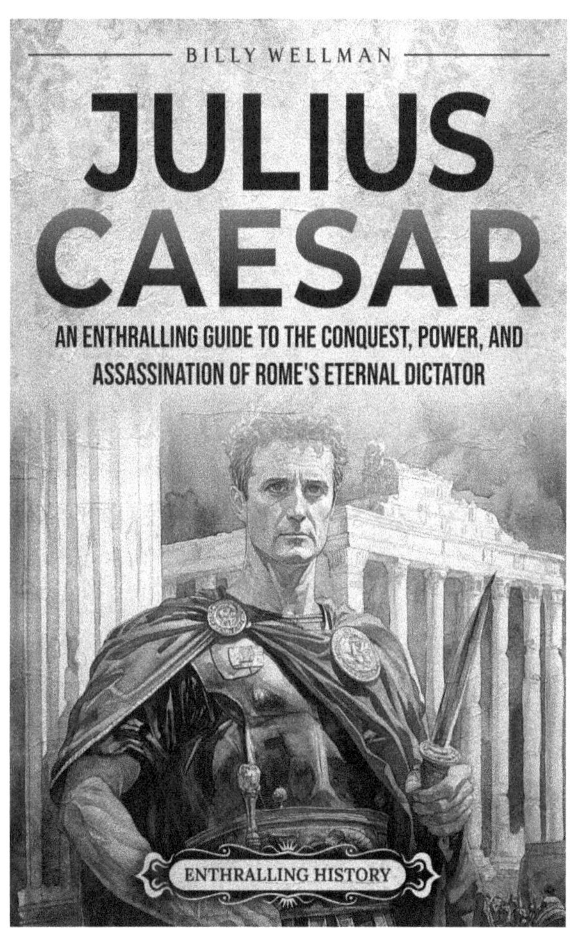

Introduction

This book is the history of the astonishing life and times of Julius Caesar. It is filled with battles, sieges, conspiracies, and assassinations. The work is perfect for beginners and even those knowledgeable about the topic. It presents Caesar in a new way so modern people can understand the Roman world through themes that are relevant today, such as democracy and authoritarianism.

Explore the remarkable personality of Caesar and his scandalous life. Learn about his political maneuvering and his great affair with Cleopatra. See how Roman culture and society shaped him into the man he became.

Discover Caesar's greatest battles, and learn about his strategic genius. You will see how Caesar came to be regarded as one of the greatest generals of all time. After all, he conquered much of western Europe and beat foreign and Roman enemies.

This work does not gloss over the darker side of Caesar either. It talks about his many crimes, such as the massacres of Germanic tribes. This work presents one of history's greatest generals as his contemporaries would have seen him.

Such a remarkable man has had a tremendous impact. You will learn how Caesar, through his many and varied conquests, laid the foundation for Europe and paved the way for the zenith of Roman power. It also shows how he was a master of propaganda and how he inspired dictators and authoritarian figures, even in the modern day.

Chapter 1: The Young Julius Caesar

The Early Years of the Future Conqueror

Julius Caesar was born into an aristocratic, or patrician, Roman family. There is no agreement on Caesar's birthday, but most believe it was July 12th, 100 BCE. His family was a member of the prestigious clan of *gens* Julia, which had an illustrious history. They claimed to have immigrated to Rome many centuries prior and originated in the fabled city of Alba Longa, which a Roman king once destroyed. The Julii also claimed descent from Julus, a son of the Trojan hero Aeneas, one of the most important figures in Roman mythology. This dubious claim meant the clan descended from a great hero and had divine origins. Aeneas was the son of the Roman goddess of love, Venus. The pedigree of the Julii was well known and added to their prestige.

As one of the old patrician families, they could claim to be members of the original aristocracy. They were distinct from the plebeian families, which had only fully integrated into the Roman aristocracy by Caesar's time. The patrician and plebeian split in the aristocracy contributed to the rivalry between the populares and the optimates factions, which dominated politics in Rome. In traditional societies such as Rome, an ancient pedigree added to a family's prestige and often translated into political influence and the ability to win elections for major magistracies, such as that of consul (one of the highest elected public offices in the Roman Republic). Roman Patrician families can be likened to modern-day political families with significant influence.

Only in the 3rd century BCE did the family become politically important. The first consul with the name Caesar was listed in 157 BCE. Two Julii consuls were elected in the 90s BCE, including Caesar's uncle Sextus. Despite this, the family was not considered one of the greatest families, and in the decades before Caesar was born, they had lost some of their prestige and influence. Caesar's father, Gaius Julius Caesar, was a member of the Roman Senate and held the office of praetor in the 90s BCE. Julius's aunt was married to Marius, an important Roman figure who defeated a massive German barbarian invasion in the Cimbrian War (113–101 BCE). He is widely credited with reforming the military and creating the Roman military machine, but some historians reject this idea.

Marius was a "new man" whose family was not originally Roman and had only recently become prominent in the city. As a new man, Marius was sympathetic to the populares party. The populares and optimates were the two dominant factions in Roman politics, though they did not really function like modern political parties. They were more like opposing ideologies held by senators. The optimates, whose name roughly translates as "the best men," represented the conservative senatorial elite. They favored preserving the traditional power of the Senate and resisted efforts to redistribute land or extend political rights more broadly. The populares sought to bypass the Senate by appealing directly to the popular assemblies, the bodies in which ordinary Roman citizens had a voice. They generally supported land reform and greater political inclusion for plebeians and Italian citizens.

The divide was as much about power and self-interest as it was about genuine ideology. Many populares came from aristocratic backgrounds themselves, and their championing of the common people was often a means of outmaneuvering their rivals in the Senate.

Marius's belief in merit was welcomed by ordinary citizens. Politics was a family business in Rome, so Julius Caesar's future political sympathies often lay with the populares. This was not as strange as it appears. The Julii had lost status and wealth, and by associating with the "new men," they hoped to regain lost ground. They could not afford to be conservative and snobbish, given their waning influence and potential financial difficulties. The wealthy patrician families would not fully accept them because of their relative lack of wealth. Moreover, like many influential families, they believed that the populares had the best interests of Rome at heart, unlike the optimates, who only wanted more land and power.

We know little about Caesar's childhood. It can be safely assumed that he was given a traditional upbringing and education. His mother, Aurelia, was a member of the powerful Cotta family and molded her son's character while providing him with support. Despite coming from a privileged background, his upbringing sought to toughen him both physically and mentally. The aim of his education was to enable him to succeed in Rome's competitive world and advance his family's interests. He would have been educated by enslaved or freed tutors and taught Latin, Greek, and rhetoric. Later in life, he was considered very cultured and even wrote verses. As a teenager, he would have studied Roman law and oratory, or the art of persuasion. He excelled at the latter, as he was considered to be a great orator, which was a factor in his political success.

Like every other aristocratic male Roman, the young Julius Caesar was expected to enter into a political and military career. At the age of sixteen, he assumed the toga, symbolizing his entry into manhood and assuming his civic responsibilities. As a young aristocrat, he was expected to advance the interests of his formerly illustrious family. In the Julii household, the masks of his dead relatives were hung. He would have seen the busts of his ancestors, such as Aeneas. The young Caesar would have been expected to equal, if not surpass, their feats. This need for recognition and respect was what drove him during his life.

The Roman Republic's extent around 100 BCE. ([28]

The origin of the name Caesar is itself a matter of some debate. The most popular explanation, and the one that has endured into modern times, is that it derived from the Latin word for a surgical birth. According to this tradition, an ancestor of Julius was delivered by what we now call a caesarean section, and the family took its name from it. This is almost certainly a myth. In the ancient world, caesarean sections were only performed when the mother was already dead or dying, as the procedure was fatal for her. Since Caesar's mother, Aurelia, not only survived his birth but lived long enough to play a significant role in his upbringing, this explanation does not hold up in the case of Julius.

Other theories have been proposed over the centuries. Some ancient writers suggested the name derived from a Punic word for elephant, after an ancestor supposedly killed one in battle. Others connected it to a word meaning a thick head of hair, which would be somewhat ironic given Caesar's well-documented sensitivity about his own baldness in later life. Unfortunately, the true origin of the name is lost to history.

Dangerous Times

The best way for young aristocrats to achieve their ambitions was through public service and following the *cursus honorum*, which involved securing high offices after demonstrating their ability. Caesar was an ardent admirer of his uncle Marius and looked to him as a role model in many ways. Based on his later career, it seems that Caesar learned from Marius that real power lay in the military and that old traditions could be easily set aside. He also learned from him that any successful politician needed the public's support.

Julius was also inspired by Alexander the Great and wanted to be a conqueror from his early years. Later writers believed that Alexander had inspired him to become the ruler of Rome. However, this is unlikely, as Caesar would have learned, as part of his education, that kings were not acceptable to the freedom-loving Romans.

Perhaps Caesar's greatest motivation was his desire for *dignitas*, honor and widespread respect. Throughout his career, his obsession was to earn more and more glory to enhance his dignitas. For Caesar, dignitas meant having a good reputation, which would ensure that his name would live forever. He was eager to secure more power, which ultimately led him to become the dictator of Rome.

The sources are fragmentary, but he possibly became engaged to or even married a young lady called Cossutia, the daughter of a wealthy equestrian (the property-owning class below the senatorial class), at the age of sixteen. This was not a love match but a practical arrangement between two families. If the two did marry, Caesar later left her to marry another. His union with Cossutia produced no children.

Young Caesar entered public life at a perilous time. The Roman Republic, in the aftermath of the Second Punic War, had secured a Mediterranean empire. Its lands stretched from Spain across the central Mediterranean into Greece and western Asia Minor and also included territories in North Africa. The Roman Republic had become prosperous, but inequality, competition among the aristocrats, and corruption led to social unrest and divisions. Increasingly, the aristocrats, or optimates, were expanding their landholdings at the expense of small citizen farmers, making land reform a subject of controversy. The optimates had twice defeated an attempt at land reform by the Gracchi brothers in the late 2nd century BCE.

The rapid expansion of the Republic after the defeat of the Carthaginians placed tremendous strain on the government and bureaucracy. Rome's government and constitution had been designed for a city-state, not a large empire. Without oversight, many governors acted like monarchs and became notorious for corruption. Increasingly, the legions owed their allegiance to their military commanders rather than to Rome. Moreover, after the Social War (91–88 BCE), a war fought between Rome and its autonomous allies in Italy, many Italians became citizens, upsetting the balance between plebeians and patricians and leading to intense political infighting. In addition, the wealth of the provinces was used by politicians to secure support, making politics even more competitive and bloody.

Civil War and Political Violence

In 84 BCE, Lucius Cornelius Cinna was serving his fourth consecutive consulship, having dominated Roman politics since 87. Around this time, Caesar's father, Gaius Julius Caesar, died (probably in 85 or 84 BCE). He had been a praetor and later governed the province of Asia. His death left the teenage Julius as head of his household.

To most Romans, Caesar would have still seemed a young man with limited immediate prospects. The Julii were an ancient patrician family, but they were not among the most dominant political houses of the period and had not produced a consul in decades. Even so, Caesar had important connections. Gaius Marius, one of the most famous generals of his day, was his uncle by marriage, having married Caesar's aunt Julia. These ties mattered. Roman politics ran on wealth, reputation, and networks of obligation. Patronage shaped elections and careers. Later in life, Caesar would build vast patronage networks of his own.

For someone who would become one of Rome's greatest generals, Caesar first entered public life not as a soldier but as a priest. In the 80s BCE, he was appointed to the priesthood of Jupiter, the Flamen Dialis. The position came with heavy religious taboos and restrictions. For instance, the Flamen Dialis could not leave Italy, could not ride a horse, and was effectively barred from military command. These were serious limits in a society that rewarded ambition and battlefield success. However, Caesar did not hold the office for long, as the civil war soon disrupted the arrangement.

Soon after earning this position, the young Caesar married Cornelia, the daughter of Cinna. This marriage also would have been more about politics and binding two families together than any true love. By marrying Cinna's daughter, Caesar aligned himself with the ruling faction in Rome. That alignment would later put him in danger.

The 80s BCE were marked by civil war. Marius and Cinna seized control of Rome after driving out their opponents. Populares and optimates competed fiercely for power. Sulla, one of the Roman Republic's most accomplished generals and a leading figure among the conservative aristocracy, was at the time commanding an army at Nola in southern Italy. He had been appointed to lead the war against Mithridates VI of Pontus, whose forces had seized Roman territory in Asia Minor and encouraged revolts across the eastern Mediterranean. In 88 BCE, however, the political struggle in Rome took a dramatic turn. Through the efforts of Marius and his allies, the command against Mithridates was transferred from Sulla to Marius.

Rather than accept the decision, Sulla took an unprecedented step. He ordered his legions to march on Rome itself. No Roman general had ever led a standing army against the city before. This act shattered a long-standing political taboo and showed how deeply military loyalty had begun to shift from the state to individual commanders.

Sulla seized Rome by force, drove his opponents into exile, and reasserted control over the government. Once the situation in the city had temporarily stabilized, he left Italy to lead the Eastern campaign. Sulla confronted Mithridates VI, whose expansion had included the massacre of thousands of Romans and Italians in Asia and the occupation of key Greek cities such as Athens. The war was brutal and destructive, especially in Greece, where several cities were besieged and sacked before Sulla eventually forced Mithridates into a settlement.

While Sulla was away, the Marian regime carried out violent reprisals against its enemies. Political killings were common, and the atmosphere in Rome was tense and unstable. Caesar, who was still very young and connected by marriage to Cinna, was not a central actor in these events.

Marius, who was already seventy years old, soon died. Cinna was later killed in a mutiny by his own soldiers. When Sulla returned from the East, he defeated the remaining opposition and again took Rome by force. Though resistance continued in places like Spain, where Sertorius maintained a rival Marian stronghold, Rome itself fell firmly under Sulla's control.

Bust of Julius Caesar as a youth. [29]

Danger and Opportunities

Sulla wanted to preserve the old order and punish those who had challenged it. He drew up lists of his political enemies—the infamous proscriptions—condemning hundreds to death and ordering their property seized. A reign of terror began in the city, and men of all ranks died. Historians have likened this period to a counter-revolution.

The newly married Julius was in grave danger. He was Marius's nephew by marriage and Cinna's son-in-law. Sulla ordered him to divorce his wife, Cornelia. Remarkably, the young man refused. As a consequence, Sulla stripped him of his priesthood of Jupiter and confiscated Cornelia's dowry. Caesar went into hiding, moving between places while reportedly suffering from a severe fever. According to ancient sources, his family, fellow priests, and even the Vestal Virgins interceded on his behalf.

Some ancient sources claim Caesar was placed on the proscription lists, though modern historians doubt this. He appears to have been targeted and threatened without being formally condemned, though. Eventually, through the efforts of influential relatives and supporters, Sulla relented. He was not known for his mercy. According to legend, he warned those pleading Caesar's case that the young man would one day prove dangerous, saying there were "many Mariuses" in him.

Caesar left Rome. He was not formally exiled, but the political climate made it the safer choice. He served on the staff of Marcus Minucius Thermus, the governor of the Roman province of Asia. Caesar was sent as a diplomat to the court of Nicomedes IV, the king of Bithynia, to secure naval support. He remained there longer than expected, and his enemies later claimed he had an affair with the king. They referred to Caesar as the "Queen of Bithynia." This was almost certainly political slander. There is no credible evidence to support a relationship between the two, but his prolonged stay certainly gave the rumors room to spread.

Caesar saw his first serious military action at the siege of Mytilene in 81 BCE. Mytilene, the principal city on the island of Lesbos, had supported Rome's enemy Mithridates VI during the First Mithridatic War and had refused to submit to Sulla's terms. Thermus moved to subdue the city, possibly in coordination with the Roman commander Lucius Licinius Lucullus. During the fighting, Caesar saved the lives of fellow soldiers. For his bravery, he was awarded the Civic Crown, one of Rome's highest military honors. It was a remarkable distinction for a young man of nineteen. Holders of the crown had the right to wear it at public occasions, a privilege that added to Caesar's growing public image.

After Mytilene, Caesar served briefly under Publius Servilius Vatia Isauricus in Cilicia, where Roman forces were engaged against pirates and local bandits. In 78 BCE, Sulla died. Caesar could now safely return to Rome. It is worth noting that, however hard the loss of his priesthood was, it had freed him from the strict taboos of the office. The restrictions placed on him with that office would have made a political and military career all but impossible. Whether Caesar would have found another path regardless is impossible to say.

A bust of Sulla.[30]

Captured by Pirates

Rome was now governed by Sulla's constitutional settlement, with his supporters firmly in control. As mentioned, Sulla believed that Rome had become unstable because ambitious politicians were appealing directly to the masses and bypassing the Senate's traditional authority. To prevent this, he strengthened the Senate's control over the government, weakened officials who represented the common people, and introduced stricter rules about how politicians could advance in their careers. His aim was to restore what he saw as the old, orderly system of aristocratic rule.

Caesar began a legal career. He made his name not by winning cases but by daring to prosecute powerful men. He brought charges against Senator Gaius Antonius Hybrida, whom the other senators accused of profiting from Sulla's proscriptions, and against a corrupt governor of Macedonia. Caesar secured no convictions in either case, but the prosecutions earned him a reputation for boldness.

To further his education, Caesar traveled to Rhodes in 75 BCE to study rhetoric and philosophy. On the way, Cilician pirates captured him and demanded a ransom for his release. According to sources, including the famous historian Plutarch, Caesar remained remarkably composed throughout his captivity. He kept to his routines, wrote poetry, and even played dice with his captors. When he learned they had demanded twenty talents for his release, he reportedly told them he was worth fifty. He also promised, apparently in earnest, that he would have them crucified when he was free. They took this as a joke. It was not. After his ransom was paid, he gathered a small force, hunted down his captors, and crucified them. This story spread and added to Caesar's growing reputation in Rome.

Caesar then continued to Rhodes, a renowned center of learning in the Hellenistic world. He improved his oratory and developed a style that contemporaries found persuasive. Some ancient sources suggest he was also exposed to Epicurean ideas during this period, though whether he studied the philosophy in a formal manner is unclear. Epicureanism states that the highest good is the absence of pain and disturbance rather than the pursuit of pleasure in the conventional sense. Some of Caesar's later statements have led historians to speculate that Epicureanism left an impression on him, but we do not know this for sure.

His studies were interrupted by the outbreak of the Third Mithridatic War, commonly dated to 73 to 63 BCE. Rome's long-standing enemy, Mithridates VI of Pontus, again moved to expand his influence in the eastern Mediterranean. Some sources suggest Caesar became involved in the early stages of the war. He appears to have raised a small local force in Asia Minor and used it against forces aligned with Mithridates, though this was not a major action. After a brief period, he returned to Rome. A political career was Caesar's priority, and Rome was where that career would be made.

Chapter 2: Caesar's Rise to Power

Caesar: Priest and Politician

Sulla died in 78 BCE, but his reforms remained in place. His supporters, the optimates, held firm control of the Senate and the major offices of state. The key target of Sulla's reforms had been the tribunate. The tribunate was the office held by the tribunes of the plebs. Each year, several tribunes were elected to represent ordinary Romans and protect them from abuses by powerful nobles. They could propose laws to the people and veto decisions made by other officials, including the Senate. Because tribunes had the power to block government actions, the office became a powerful political weapon. Sulla weakened the tribunate by stripping those tribunes of much of their authority, making it far harder for them to challenge the Senate.

This was the central grievance of those who opposed Sulla's settlement. No one wanted a return to civil war, but the political struggle to dismantle his reforms continued. The resistance came from multiple factions, not simply the populares, though they were among the most vocal. Some wanted the powers of the tribunes restored, arguing that Sulla had silenced the voice of the people and handed too much authority to the Senate. Ambitious young nobles resented the fact that these reforms limited their advancement, and wealthy non-senators wanted influence in the courts returned to them.

In 73 BCE, Caesar was appointed to the College of Pontiffs, becoming a pontifex. This was a prestigious office, increasing his public standing and influence considerably. Around the same time, he was elected military tribune, a common early step for young aristocrats. Military tribunes served as staff officers and junior commanders rather than independent field commanders. It was a useful position for building connections and creating visibility.

The Third Servile War broke out in 73 BCE when enslaved people led by Spartacus rebelled and ravaged much of southern Italy. The revolt was ultimately crushed by Marcus Licinius Crassus, with the famous general Pompey playing a supporting role in its final stages. Caesar did not play any meaningful part in suppressing the rebellion, but he did begin to develop a relationship with Crassus during this period. Crassus would later prove important to his career.

Caesar used his connection to Marius publicly and aligned himself with those pushing to reverse Sulla's reforms. He also became a vocal supporter of Pompey, who was, at that point, the most prominent Roman general. However, Pompey had a history of fighting against the Marian cause. Pompey had helped defeat Sertorius in Spain, who had established an independent state loyal to the Marian faction, and had suppressed the revolt of Lepidus in 77 BCE when the consul attempted to overturn Sulla's settlement by force. Nevertheless, Caesar recognized that Pompey's military prestige made him a powerful political force.

In 70 BCE, Pompey and Crassus were elected consuls. Both opposed key elements of Sulla's constitution. During their consulship, the powers of the tribunate were largely restored. Caesar's influence was rising steadily during this period, building his support base through charm, ambition, and strategic alliances. He was not yet a major political player, but he was becoming a recognizable figure in Roman public life.

The First Triumvirate. Left to right is Pompey, Crassus, and Caesar[31]

Masterful Politician

Caesar's connections, oratory, and political maneuvering allowed him to gain higher offices. In 69 BCE, he was elected quaestor. The office required him to serve under the proprietor (governor) of Hispania Ulterior in southern Spain. However, his time there was cut short by two deaths. His aunt Julia, the widow of Marius, died, as did his wife Cornelia, who had recently given birth to his only daughter, Julia. Caesar returned to Rome to deliver both eulogies. At his aunt's funeral, he displayed images of Marius in public, something that had not been done since Sulla's victory in the civil war. It made him popular with ordinary Romans but caused considerable anger among senators who had suffered under Marius.

Ancient sources also record an anecdote from Caesar's time in Spain. While in what is now Cádiz, Caesar reportedly saw a statue of Alexander the Great and wept, struck by how much the Macedonian had accomplished at a young age. The story is reported by Plutarch but cannot be verified, so it may be a later invention.

Caesar's election as quaestor made him eligible to sit in the Senate. After Cornelia's death, he eventually married Pompeia, doing so around 67 BCE. Pompeia was connected to the family of Sulla, and the match may have been seen as a gesture of reconciliation between Caesar and the conservative Cornelii clan. The marriage produced no children, and Caesar started to become notorious during this period for his extramarital affairs.

In 65 BCE, he was elected curule aedile. The office gave him responsibility for the day-to-day administration of Rome and allowed him to act as a patron to a large number of clients. Patronage was central to Roman political life, and many of the ties Caesar cultivated during this period remained loyal to him throughout his career. He organized lavish games, such as gladiatorial combat, animal hunts, and other popular entertainment, which made him enormously popular with the Roman public. As you could probably guess, a political career was expensive, and Caesar fell heavily into debt financing his ambitions. He also restored the trophies and images of Marius, a move that his enemies attacked in the Senate.

Around the same time, the Senate passed the Lex Gabinia in 67 BCE, granting Pompey sweeping powers to deal with the pirate threat. Pirates, operating mainly from Cilicia, had disrupted Rome's grain supply and coastal trade to a serious degree. This law gave Pompey authority over any area within fifty miles of the sea, the ability to raise funds, and the power to appoint legates without consultation. It was an extraordinary grant of power. Pompey moved quickly and crushed the pirates in a matter of months. Then, in 66 BCE, the Lex Manilia granted him command of the Roman legions in the East, replacing Lucius Licinius Lucullus, whose exhausted troops had become increasingly resistant to further campaigning. Caesar supported both measures, though many did so. Pompey went on to defeat Mithridates and extend Roman power as far as Judea. It was during this period that he became known as Pompey the Great.

In 63 BCE, Caesar sought election as Pontifex Maximus, the chief priest of Rome. He would be responsible for overseeing the city's religious observances and traditions. It was a highly prestigious office. Among his rivals was the conservative senator Catulus. Caesar's candidacy was met with some skepticism. Despite his priestly office, he was not known for his piety, and his outlook on religion was more rationalistic, which was common among educated Romans of his class. He won regardless. His enemies claimed he had bribed the electors, which was entirely possible. Although Caesar had fallen deeply into debt by this point, bribery and vote-buying were a standard feature of Roman political life. He was far from alone in practicing this. The title Pontifex Maximus was later passed to Roman emperors and was eventually adopted by the bishop of Rome.

A bust of Cicero.[32]

That same year, he was elected praetor for 62 BCE, one of the Roman Republic's senior offices. This double victory showed that, despite growing suspicion among conservatives, he had built a real following in Rome.

Political Scandal and Conspiracy

If Caesar was expecting an easy time, he was wrong. The year 62 BCE proved to be a turbulent year for him. As Pontifex Maximus, he and his household resided in the official residence on the Via Sacra. His wife Pompeia had religious duties that included hosting the Festival of the Bona Dea, a ceremony restricted to women. The notorious Publius

Clodius allegedly disguised himself as a woman and entered the house during the festival. The scandal was huge. Clodius was arrested and charged with impiety. Caesar declined to testify against him and did not pursue a prosecution. He did, however, divorce Pompeia. When asked why, he reportedly said that his wife must be above suspicion—a phrase that has passed into common usage. By divorcing Pompeia, he distanced himself from the scandal and signaled that any impropriety was unacceptable in his household.

The same year saw the Catilinarian conspiracy. Lucius Sergius Catilina (better known in English as simply Catiline), having failed to win the consulship, gathered a force of supporters and attempted to overthrow the elected government. The conspiracy was uncovered by the consul Cicero, who moved swiftly against it. The ringleaders in Rome, including Lentulus and Cethegus, were arrested. Catiline himself fled and was killed in battle in 62 BCE.

In the Senate, Caesar spoke in favor of caution. He argued against the summary execution of the conspirators held in Rome on the grounds that it would be controversial. The Senate's emergency decree, the *senatus consultum ultimum*, gave broad powers, but it did not explicitly extend to executing Roman citizens without trial, making this a matter of genuine legal dispute. Caesar proposed instead that the conspirators be detained in Italian towns and their property confiscated. It was an unusual proposal. Rome did not typically use long-term detention as a punishment, and the logistics would be difficult. Cato the Younger argued forcefully for execution and prevailed. The conspirators were put to death.

Caesar's enemies claimed he had been involved in the conspiracy itself. This was almost certainly political slander. Some modern scholars have questioned aspects of Cicero's account and whether the threat was as grave as he presented it, but most believe that the conspiracy was real. Caesar's opposition to the executions was more likely rooted in legal principle and political calculation than in sympathy for them. His stance earned him some new supporters and presented him as a voice for moderation at a time when Romans had grown weary of political violence. Whether it won him more than it cost him is difficult to say. He was still a controversial figure by the end of 62 BCE. He had built a broad support base, but many conservatives deeply distrusted him.

Battles in Spain

After his praetorship, Caesar was appointed governor of Hispania Ulterior, where he had previously served as quaestor. He governed with proconsular imperium, though his formal rank was propraetor. Proconsular imperium is the legal authority given to Roman officers to govern provinces outside of Rome. He commanded the provincial forces available to him and raised additional troops as needed. It was his first independent military command. He had watched how Pompey and Marius had built their careers on military reputation, and he needed victories and money. A provincial command offered both.

Roman control over the Iberian Peninsula was well established in most areas, though the northwest remained less firmly under Roman authority. Caesar moved against the tribes of that region. Among them were the Gallaeci, who inhabited what is now Galicia in the northwest. He invaded their territory using a combination of land forces and a fleet to maintain supply lines, moving quickly through difficult terrain. He subdued the Gallaeci and pushed on to the Atlantic coast. He also campaigned against the Lusitanians in what is now Portugal, subduing them as well. These victories led his troops to hail him as imperator, a title given to a successful general and a necessary step toward claiming a triumph in Rome. He exaggerated the significance of his victories somewhat—the northwest was not fully pacified—but they still enhanced his standing in Rome.

His victories also qualified him for a triumph. This presented a problem. To celebrate a triumph, a general had to remain outside the city boundary, the *pomerium,* until the ceremony. But to declare his candidacy for the consulship, he had to appear in person in Rome. He could not do both. His conservative opponents, led by Cato the Younger, refused any accommodation and insisted that Caesar abide by tradition. Caesar chose the consulship and abandoned the triumph. It was a pragmatic decision, though it added to his grievances against Cato and the conservative faction.

Rise to Power

Caesar declared his candidacy for the consulship of 59 BCE. The field included several candidates. Caesar campaigned effectively. His oratory was persuasive, and he had support across different factions, in part because he had presented himself as a moderate rather than a partisan. He needed money, though, so he turned to Crassus. He also sought to coordinate with Lucius Lucceius, a wealthy aristocrat who was also running for consul, in hopes of pooling resources. Ultimately, Caesar won. The second consulship went to Bibulus, a staunch conservative and political opponent of Caesar, which complicated matters from the start.

Before taking office, Caesar had already set about building the political foundation he would need. Crassus and Pompey distrusted each other and had clashed before. So, Caesar brokered an informal arrangement between them. Modern historians call this the First Triumvirate, though it was not officially recognized by the Senate. It was a private practical alliance. Pompey brought military prestige and veteran soldiers who needed land. Crassus brought money. Caesar brought political skill, popular support, and his connections with the populares. He was the least powerful of the three in military terms, but he was the one who made the alliance function. Also, as Pontifex Maximus, Caesar held Rome's highest religious office. While magistrates were the ones who formally consulted omens before public meetings, his position still gave him influence over religious matters that could affect politics.

Caesar had come a long way. Until this point, his career had been more political than military. That was about to change.

Chapter 3: First Consulship and the Gallic Wars

Caesar's Political Genius

Caesar used his consulship to push through significant reforms. The Roman constitution required laws to be passed by the popular assemblies rather than the Senate, though Senate support was essential to pass anything. The alliance with Crassus and Pompey gave him the muscle to overcome the factional deadlock that had blocked reform for years.

He had the Senate's proceedings published for the first time, making its business visible to ordinary Romans. Pompey needed land for his veterans, and Caesar delivered it with a land distribution bill. Crassus wanted relief for his tax-farming clients in the provinces, and Caesar adjusted the taxation system. In return, both men backed his consulship.

Conservatives in the Senate, led by Cato the Younger, bitterly opposed all of it. Caesar's fellow consul, Bibulus, attempted to block the legislation through obstruction and by invoking religious technicalities, declaring that the omens were unfavorable and that no public business could lawfully proceed. Caesar ignored these declarations and pressed ahead, bringing his land bill before the popular assembly. Tensions quickly escalated. When Bibulus tried to intervene in person, violence broke out among the crowd. His attendants were attacked, and Bibulus was forced to flee. Humiliated and unable to stop Caesar, Bibulus withdrew to his house, where he spent the remainder of the year issuing formal protests that were largely ignored.

The First Triumvirate dominated Roman politics that year, though significant opposition remained. Caesar cemented his relationship with Pompey further by giving him his daughter Julia in marriage. It seemed the two men had a genuinely close bond.

During his consulship, Caesar also passed the Lex Julia de Repetundis, a law cracking down on corruption in the provinces. Governors had long been accused of exploiting the people under their rule, enriching themselves at Rome's expense. Caesar's law tightened the rules and made it easier to prosecute those who abused their power. It was one of his more lasting achievements, surviving long after many of his other controversial measures had faded.

When his consulship ended, Caesar moved quickly to secure his position. He and his supporters passed a law granting him an extraordinary provincial command. He would have proconsular authority over Illyricum, Cisalpine Gaul, and Transalpine Gaul with a term of five years. Multi-year commands were not entirely without precedent—Pompey had received similar arrangements—but the combination of three provinces and multiple legions was unusual. Caesar left for these provinces as soon as his consulship expired. As a private citizen in Rome, he would have been vulnerable to prosecution by his enemies, and Cato the Younger had made it clear that he intended to pursue exactly that. Leaving was the safer option.

Also in 59 BCE, Caesar married Calpurnia, his third wife. She came from the powerful Piso family. Like his previous marriages, it was a political arrangement. It strengthened his ties with an important family at an important moment.

Map of Gaul during Caesar's invasion[33]

The War with the Germans

Caesar already held command of his provinces before any Gallic crisis emerged. When the opportunity for war presented itself the following year, he took it. Under Roman tradition, war had to be just. It had to be fought in defense of Rome or its allies. Caesar found his justification in the movements of the Helvetii, a Celtic people from what is now Switzerland, who migrated westward into Gaul in 58 BCE, allegedly under pressure from Germanic tribes to the east. Their migration threatened the Aedui, a tribe allied with Rome. Caesar intervened, framing the campaign as a defense of Roman allies rather than outright conquest.

He expanded his forces before moving against the Helvetii, raising additional legions. He intercepted them near Bibracte and positioned his legions on high ground with the baggage train behind them. The Helvetii attacked directly. The legions' throwing javelins broke up the assault, and even the arrival of allied reinforcements, including the Boii, could not turn the tide. The Helvetii were defeated and forced to return to their homeland. They retained a degree of autonomy but were now effectively subordinate to Rome.

Caesar then turned north. The Suebi, a Germanic people under their leader Ariovistus, had invaded the territory of the Aedui and the Sequani, pushing deep into Gaul. Ariovistus had previously been recognized by the Senate as a friend of Rome, but his continued expansion threatened Roman interests. Caesar marched his legions into Sequani territory. Negotiations were attempted, but they quickly broke down.

Ariovistus proved to be a capable strategist. He maneuvered his army behind the Roman forces, threatening their supply lines. For several days, neither side would commit to open battle. Eventually, his warriors, eager to fight, forced his hand. The Germans attacked. Their initial charge pushed the Roman lines hard. Caesar ordered the cavalry under Publius Crassus, the son of his ally, to strike at the exposed German flank. That charge broke their formation, and Roman infantry discipline did the rest. The Suebi were driven back across the Rhine.

Caesar reported that 120,000 of the enemy were killed. Modern historians treat such figures with considerable skepticism. Ancient commanders routinely inflated enemy losses, and Caesar would have been no exception. What is not in doubt is that in a single year, he had defeated two large forces and significantly extended Roman influence in Gaul.

Caesar was also a skilled propagandist. He sent regular dispatches back to Rome, where they were circulated and read publicly. These accounts were later compiled into the *Commentarii de Bello Gallico* (*Commentaries of the Gallic War*). They are considered a masterpiece of Latin prose. They are also, without question, a work of political self-promotion. Caesar's victories are presented in the best possible light, with his setbacks minimized or omitted entirely.

The Conquest of Gaul

Caesar returned to Transalpine Gaul, where he rested his troops, raised new recruits, and attended to the administration of his provinces. He also enlisted Gallic and German auxiliaries to supplement his cavalry. After the victories of 58 BCE, much of Gaul appeared open to conquest. And once again, local disputes gave him a reason to intervene.

The Belgae, a large tribal confederation inhabiting what is now Belgium and the surrounding region, began raiding a Roman ally. What made this threat unusual was its scale. The Belgic tribes had formed a rare intertribal coalition, and Caesar reported their combined numbers as enormous. These figures were almost certainly exaggerated, but they allowed him to present the campaign as defending Roman security rather than outright aggression. Caesar moved quickly. He marched to the main settlement of the Remi, a tribe that had allied itself with Rome, with a force of up to twenty thousand legionaries and an unknown number of allied troops.

The two sides faced each other across the River Aisne in a tense standoff. Caesar fortified his position and refused to be drawn into unfavorable ground. The Belgic coalition was vast and began to fracture. Shortages and internal divisions forced them to dissolve before a decisive engagement could take place.

Caesar pressed forward into Belgic territory anyway, despite dangerously overstretched supply lines. He laid siege to one of the tribe's major hillforts. The defenders, unfamiliar with Roman siege equipment, surrendered. Caesar then prudently withdrew to Roman-held territory.

On the return march, the legions were ambushed by the Nervii, one of the most formidable of the Belgic tribes, along with their allies. The Nervii struck while the Romans were still making camp, driving back the cavalry and light troops before the legions could form properly. The fighting was desperate, and Roman centurions fell in significant numbers. The lines came close to breaking entirely. Caesar took a shield and fought in the front ranks himself, a move that steadied his men. Fighting alongside their commander let them know that the battle could be won. Other Roman units that had advanced too far returned to the field in time to help. It was one of the most dangerous moments of Caesar's entire Gallic command. The Nervii were eventually defeated, but the battle showed how formidable Rome's enemies in the north could be.

The defeat of the Nervii broke the wider Belgic resistance. Most tribes submitted under harsh terms. The Aduatuci, who refused, were dealt with ruthlessly. Caesar claims tens of thousands were sold into slavery. The sale of captives generated enormous wealth for Caesar and his officers. Some Germanic tribes along the Rhine sought diplomatic contact with Rome, though the frontier remained unstable.

The year 57 BCE had been another year of significant victories. Caesar wintered his army in northern Gaul. The following year brought fresh trouble. Roman taxation and demands had pushed many Gallic tribes toward rebellion. The leaders of the revolt were the Veneti, a maritime people of what is now Brittany. They had detained Roman envoys, and they controlled the Atlantic trade routes of western Gaul. Their coastal hillforts made them almost impossible to subdue by land alone. If they were besieged in one, they could simply escape by sea to another.

Caesar needed a fleet. He forced his allies to help him build one capable of operating in Atlantic waters. The two fleets met in Quiberon Bay. The Roman ships were oar-powered, while the Veneti relied on sail. Caesar's sailors used hooks on long poles to catch and cut the Veneti rigging, disabling their ships and leaving them vulnerable to boarding. The Veneti, caught without wind and unable to maneuver, were overwhelmed. This is a great example of Roman adaptability, as Caesar had never commanded a fleet before. The defeat of the Veneti extended Rome's reach to the Atlantic coast and intimidated the remaining coastal tribes. Their leadership was executed, and the survivors were sold into slavery. Caesar's subordinates, including Publius Crassus, continued operations in the southwest and Normandy.

Much of Gaul had now submitted, at least formally. Caesar's army was becoming something more than a provincial force. It was battle-hardened, experienced in a dozen different kinds of terrain and enemy, and increasingly loyal to its commander rather than to Rome. That bond would matter greatly in the years ahead.

In 56 BCE, Caesar met with Crassus and Pompey at Lucca to renew their alliance. The meeting drew around two hundred senators. The three men agreed to support each other's ambitions. Pompey and Crassus would stand for the consulship again. Crassus would receive Syria, where the prospect of a war against the Parthians, a powerful Iranian empire, loomed. Pompey would receive Spain. Caesar's own command in Gaul was extended for another five years. This was no minor thing. It guaranteed continued imperium, which protected him from prosecution, and gave him the time and resources to complete the conquest.

However, tensions within the alliance were already growing. Conservative senators, Cato among them, were working to draw Pompey away from Caesar. Pompey still commanded enormous prestige in Rome. But Caesar's victories, and the wealth and loyalty they had generated, had made him a force that could no longer be ignored.

Crossing the Rhine and the First Invasion of England

In 55 BCE, Germanic tribes crossed the Rhine into Gaul, threatening the stability Caesar had spent years establishing. Rather than simply repel them, he decided to make a statement. He ordered his engineers to build a bridge across the Rhine. His men would not use boats; this would be a proper timber bridge driven into the riverbed. It was completed in ten days, stretching across one of the greatest rivers of the known world. Caesar crossed with his army and spent eighteen days raiding Germanic territory. He and his men burned the villages of tribes that refused to submit and then withdrew, demolishing the bridge behind them. Caesar had never intended to stay. The point was the crossing itself. He wanted to show the Germanic tribes that the Rhine was not a barrier to Roman power and that no one was beyond his reach.

That same year, Caesar made his first crossing to Britain. He took two legions, although they achieved little beyond a landing on the coast. They were forced back by storms and determined British resistance. It was, by his own standards, an unsatisfying result. Caesar returned the following year, 54 BCE, with a much larger force–five legions and two thousand cavalry carried in eight hundred ships. It was the largest amphibious operation in the history of the world at that point.

This time, the landing was unopposed. The Britons united under a capable warlord named Cassivellaunus, who realized he could not defeat Caesar in open battle and instead used chariot warfare and guerrilla tactics to slow the Roman advance. Caesar forced a crossing of the Thames, pushing into Cassivellaunus's territory north of the river. Rival British tribes, hostile to Cassivellaunus, provided intelligence that led Caesar to his stronghold.

Faced with the fall of his base and pressure from multiple directions, Cassivellaunus sued for peace. He handed over hostages and agreed to pay an annual tribute. Caesar left without leaving a single soldier behind. Whether the tribute was ever paid is unknown. Britain was not conquered, but Caesar had been there and forced its leading warlord to submit. In Rome, that was enough.

Caesar returned to Gaul to find the situation deteriorating, as even Roman allies hated the burden of occupation. The legions had to be fed by the local population, who could barely feed themselves. A poor harvest had made the situation even more desperate. Caesar was forced to scatter his legions across a wide area to avoid overburdening any single tribe. This left them isolated and vulnerable.

In the winter of 54 BCE, an Eburones chieftain named Ambiorix saw his opportunity. He approached the Roman commanders Sabinus and Cotta, who were wintering in Eburones territory with a legion and five cohorts (a unit of a legion that numbered around 480 men), and deceived them with a false warning. He told them all of Gaul was rising and that Germanic tribes were crossing the Rhine. He offered safe passage if they abandoned their camp. Sabinus, against the advice of his co-commander Cotta, accepted.

It was a catastrophic mistake. As the Roman column moved out, Ambiorix's men ambushed them in a ravine. The legion was virtually destroyed. Sabinus was killed attempting to negotiate, and Cotta fell fighting. A handful of survivors made their way to other Roman camps to report the disaster.

Ambiorix then moved against Quintus Cicero, the younger brother of the famous orator, who was wintering nearby with another legion. Unlike Sabinus, Cicero refused to be deceived and held his camp under a sustained siege that lasted weeks. His men suffered enormous casualties; by the end, nine out of ten had been wounded. Caesar moved to relieve him with whatever forces he could gather, marching his men hard through Nervii territory. He arrived in time. The Gauls abandoned the siege and were driven off.

It had been the most dangerous winter of the entire Gallic campaign and served as a reminder that the conquest of Gaul was far from complete.

A modern reimagining of Caesar's bridge over the Rhine.[34]

The Revolt of Rome and Vercingetorix

In 52 BCE, a young Arvernian nobleman named Vercingetorix achieved something remarkable. He persuaded the disunited tribes of Gaul to set aside their rivalries and unite against Rome. The various tribes swore to defend their lands and drive out the invaders. It was the most serious challenge to Roman rule since Caesar had first crossed into Gaul.

Caesar was in Cisalpine Gaul when the revolt broke out. He moved with his usual quick speed, crossing into Transalpine Gaul and launching an offensive through the south before the rebel alliance could fully organize. Vercingetorix knew he could not match the Romans in open battle. His strategy was to avoid direct confrontation, destroy food supplies, and starve the legions. His allies pushed him to fight, though, and at Avaricum—one of the most prosperous towns in Gaul and one of the few his allies had refused to burn as part of their scorched-earth strategy—Caesar laid siege and eventually stormed the walls. According to his own account, most of the population was massacred. It was a brutal demonstration of what resistance cost and a warning to the rest of Gaul.

Vercingetorix withdrew to Gergovia, the hilltop stronghold of the Arverni in what is now south-central France. It was a formidable position. Caesar moved against it and began building fortifications to cut it off, though the terrain made a complete encirclement impossible. When the Aedui tribe revolted and disrupted his supply lines, Caesar's position became precarious. Rather than lift the siege, he ordered an assault. It went badly. The attack broke down in confusion, and there was poor coordination between units. The Gallic defenders inflicted heavy casualties. Caesar later claimed he had not suffered a defeat, but his losses were severe enough that he was forced to withdraw. It was the lowest point of the entire campaign.

Vercingetorix gathered his forces at Alesia, a heavily fortified settlement on a plateau in what is now Burgundy. Caesar chose not to assault it directly. Instead, he ordered the construction of an enormous ring of fortifications around the town. In the end, there were over twenty miles of trenches, walls, towers, and an elaborate system of concealed pits and sharpened stakes designed to break any sortie from the garrison. At the same time, a vast Gallic relief army assembled and marched to break the siege. Caesar's response was to build a second ring of fortifications facing outward, protecting his army from an attack in the rear. His force now sat between the garrison inside Alesia and the relief army outside. Caesar's men were under attack from both directions, and the fighting was ferocious and continuous. Whether Vercingetorix had planned from the outset to draw Caesar into this position or had simply retreated to Alesia after his earlier reverses is debated by historians.

In the end, Roman discipline and engineering proved decisive. The Gallic relief army could not break through Caesar's outer fortifications. Supplies ran out inside Alesia. In desperation, Vercingetorix sent the women and children of the town out through the gates, hoping Caesar would let them pass or be moved to negotiate. Caesar refused. Trapped in the no-man's land between the two lines, many of them died of starvation and exposure. The relief army, unable to feed itself in the field, eventually scattered. With no hope of rescue, Vercingetorix surrendered. He rode out to Caesar and laid down his arms. He was taken to Rome, where he was held prisoner for years. He was eventually executed after Caesar's triumph.

The fall of Alesia broke Gallic resistance. The remaining tribes submitted, becoming clients of Rome or coming under direct Roman administration. Caesar had conquered a vast area of western Europe in less than a decade. However, the human cost was enormous. Ancient sources claim that millions died or were enslaved during the Gallic Wars, and some modern historians have described the campaign as genocidal in scale. The precise figures are impossible to verify because ancient casualty numbers are almost always exaggerated, but few serious scholars doubt that the wars caused a devastating loss of life across the region.

Vercingetorix surrendering to Caesar.[35]

Trouble Back Home

By 53 BCE, the First Triumvirate was close to collapse. Julia, Caesar's daughter and Pompey's wife, had died in childbirth. The personal bond between the two men pretty much died with her. Each grew suspicious of the other, and the alliance that had dominated Roman politics for years began to unravel.

Crassus, meanwhile, was increasingly aware that his partners had eclipsed him in military glory. He decided to fix this with a conquest of his own. Parthia, a powerful empire on Rome's eastern frontier, was his target. Crassus had military experience; he had served under Sulla in the civil wars of the 80s BCE and had crushed Spartacus decisively. However, he lacked the strategic brilliance and adaptability of men like Pompey and Caesar.

He led a force of roughly thirty-five thousand to forty thousand men into the East. The Parthians refused to meet him in a conventional engagement. Instead, a Parthian general named Surena drew the Romans into the open desert of what is now eastern Syria, near the town of Carrhae. There, he unleashed his cavalry. The mounted archers, for which Parthia was famous, were capable of shooting at full gallop and even backward at pursuing enemies. Surena kept his archers supplied by camel train, ensuring the volleys never stopped.

The Roman formation held for a time but had no answer for the harassment. When the Romans finally broke during the retreat, the Parthians pursued and destroyed much of the army. Around twenty thousand Romans were killed, and ten thousand were taken prisoner. Several thousand escaped to Syria. The Roman legionary standards were captured; this was a profound humiliation that Rome would not avenge for decades. They were not recovered until the reign of Augustus, who obtained them through diplomacy rather than force. Crassus himself was killed during a failed negotiation. Ancient sources, including Plutarch and Cassius Dio, claim that molten gold was poured into his mouth after his death, a commentary on his greed. Whether this is true is impossible to say, although it reads more like legend than history.

The Battle of Carrhae was more than a military disaster. It removed the man who had held the First Triumvirate together. Crassus had been the third pillar of the alliance. He was wealthy enough to fund both his partners and useful as a mediator between two men whose ambitions were pulling in opposite directions. Without him, the arrangement became a contest between Caesar and Pompey.

The Senate conservatives, led by Cato and others, recognized the opportunity. They began working on Pompey, flattering him, appealing to his pride, and positioning him as the defender of the Roman Republic against Caesar's growing power. Pompey, whose relationship with the conservative bloc had always been complicated, began to move in their direction.

The process accelerated in 52 BCE. The murder of the populist agitator Clodius on the Appian Way sparked serious street violence in Rome. Clodius was no ordinary politician. A fiery populist and former tribune, he had built a powerful following among the urban poor and commanded loyal street gangs who clashed regularly with his rivals. For years, Rome's politics had spilled out of the Senate and into the streets, where intimidation and violence were becoming common tools of power. Clodius had actually helped create this atmosphere.

When he was killed in a confrontation with the followers of his rival Milo, news of his death spread quickly. His supporters carried his body into the Forum, where anger turned to fury. The crowd used benches and furniture to build a funeral pyre inside the Senate House itself, burning it to the ground.

With elections already delayed and no consuls in office, the Senate found itself unable to restore control through normal means. In desperation, it took the extraordinary step of appointing Pompey as sole consul. This was a rare and controversial move that gave Pompey sweeping authority to stabilize the city.

It is important to note that this was legally sanctioned. It was not a dictatorship, but it marked a decisive shift. Pompey was now governing Rome with the backing of the conservative Senate. His break with Caesar was no longer a gradual drift; it was becoming a political reality. Rome was dividing into two camps: Pompey, who was aligned with the Senate, and Caesar, who commanded a loyal and battle-hardened army in Gaul. Both men were very powerful. Neither trusted the other. A confrontation was becoming very difficult to avoid.

Chapter 4: Crossing the Rubicon

In northern Italy flows the River Rubicon, a name derived from the Latin *rubico,* meaning "red," likely a reference to the reddish clay or mineral sediment that discolored its waters. On the morning of January 10th, 49 BCE, Julius Caesar crossed the Rubicon at the head of the Thirteenth Legion. His biographer Suetonius records that before crossing, Caesar declared, "Iacta alea est"–"The die is cast." It was the greatest gamble of his career.

The river's significance was legal as much as geographical. It marked the boundary between Cisalpine Gaul, which Caesar governed as his province, and the territory directly under the authority of the Senate. Roman law was clear on this point. A governor's imperium–his legal authority to command troops–applied only within his province. The moment he led armed forces across that line, his immunity evaporated. He became a private citizen under military command, which the Senate could treat as treason. This mattered enormously to Caesar. As long as he held imperium, he could not be prosecuted for his actions in Gaul. The moment he laid down his command and entered Rome as a private citizen, his enemies could (and likely would) put him on trial.

Cato and the conservative faction had spent years trying to maneuver Caesar into exactly that position. In early 49 BCE, the Senate demanded that Caesar disband his legions before his command formally expired. They then issued the *senatus consultum ultimum,* the emergency decree of last resort that effectively authorized the use of force against him. Caesar had no good options left. Crossing the river with his army was illegal. Submitting to the Senate meant ruin.

Caesar chose to cross. The phrase "crossing the Rubicon" is still used as a term for the point of no return.

The Senate moved quickly but had little to work with. Pompey's best troops were in Spain, and Italy itself was largely undefended. Rather than fight, the conservative faction fled Rome. This was not pure panic. Pompey wanted to regroup in the East, where he had deep networks of client states and loyal veterans. That way, he could defeat Caesar from a position of strength. It was a rational strategy, though it ceded Italy without a fight and badly damaged morale. Caesar's subordinates seized key positions across Italy while he marched south.

The road to the Rubicon stretched back several years. As mentioned, Julia, Caesar's daughter and Pompey's wife, had died in 54 BCE, which dissolved the personal bond between the two men. In 50 BCE, Caesar proposed that both he and Pompey disband their armies, which would have removed the military threat on both sides. The Senate, under the influence of the optimates, refused unless Caesar disarmed first. Pompey would not agree to mutual disarmament.

After his victory at Alesia, Caesar had petitioned the Senate to stand for the consulship in absentia; this means he would stand for consulship without giving up his command. The Senate refused. Cato the Younger and his allies also blocked him from celebrating a triumph.

Why Caesar chose to cross rather than negotiate or submit has been debated for centuries. Ancient sources, including Suetonius and Plutarch, tend to portray it as personal ambition. This was the act of a man who had always intended to make himself master of Rome. Modern historians are less certain. Some see Caesar acting defensively, protecting his dignitas and his political survival against enemies who left him no lawful way out. Others argue that he had long sought sole power and used the legal crisis as justification. Most likely, both were true to some degree. What is clear is that the Roman Republic's institutions had been under strain for decades.

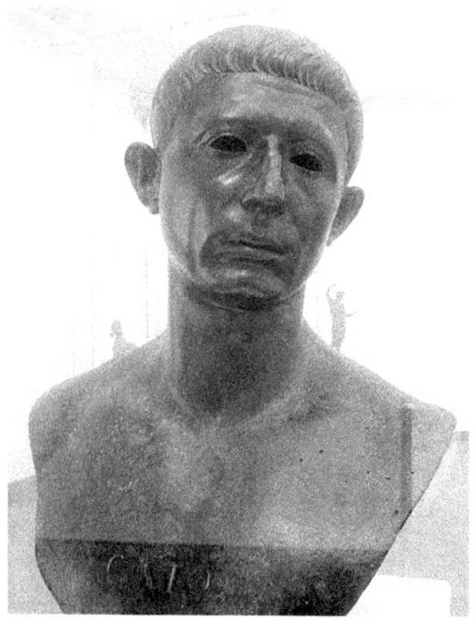

A bronze bust of Cato the Younger. [36]

Caesar's Civil War in Spain

Caesar now controlled Italy but faced Pompeian armies on multiple fronts, namely in Spain, Africa, and the Balkans. He also had to deal with Massalia, a powerful Greek city in what is now Marseille, which had declared neutrality but was effectively siding with Pompey. Caesar began the siege, left two capable generals in command to continue it, and turned his attention to Spain.

Before leaving Rome, Caesar attempted to access the state treasury to fund his campaign. A tribune named Metellus tried to block him. Caesar overrode this opposition and forced compliance. The episode was telling. Fighting a civil war was very expensive, and Caesar needed funds immediately. The treasury was the fastest source. That a tribune—theoretically a sacrosanct office, immune from force—could be brushed aside showed how far republican norms had already eroded. In Rome, Mark Antony was left in control of Italy, and Lepidus still served as praetor.

Spain was the main priority. Pompey had built his political base there over decades, and the legions in the peninsula were experienced veterans loyal to his cause. Control of Spain meant control of significant manpower and revenue—resources Caesar could not leave in enemy hands while he pursued Pompey in the East.

The Pompeian legates Lucius Afranius and Marcus Petreius held Hispania Citerior with veteran forces and had seized much of the northwest. Caesar marched quickly, raised additional troops, and moved against their position on the River Segre near Ilerda (known today as Lleida). The fighting was hard. Both sides were experienced, morale was strained, and there were even instances of soldiers from opposing sides communicating with each other. The decisive move came when Caesar ordered trenches to be dug to divert the river, threatening to cut the Pompeians off from their supply lines. Unnerved, the republican forces retreated, but Caesar surrounded them before they could reach safety. Facing no escape, the Pompeian legions surrendered. Most were disarmed and dismissed rather than incorporated into Caesar's ranks.

With Spain secured, Caesar could turn his full attention to Pompey in the East.

Siege of Massalia and the Campaign in North Africa

The siege of Massalia had continued in Caesar's absence under the command of Gaius Trebonius on land and Decimus Junius Brutus Albinus at sea. The defenders put up a determined resistance. At one point, during a negotiated truce, they set fire to the Roman siege works. This bought them time, but it did not change the outcome. The city surrendered in September 49 BCE. Caesar was not there, but he had already ordered that Massalia should not be sacked and that the inhabitants should be treated with restraint.

The situation in Africa was more damaging. The province was strategically vital for reasons that went beyond its geography. It supplied a significant portion of Rome's grain and controlled sea routes between Italy and the western Mediterranean. A hostile force based there could threaten Sicily and Italy directly. If Africa fell into Pompeian hands, it could be a base from which eastern and western forces could coordinate against Caesar. The war was already becoming an international struggle.

Caesar entrusted the African campaign to Gaius Scribonius Curio, an able politician but an inexperienced general. Curio landed with a huge force and moved against the Pompeian commander Publius Attius Varus, who held the city and port of Utica. Curio defeated Varus in battle near the city and then began a siege. The Caesarians also captured much of the enemy fleet.

However, Varus held on, knowing that help was on the way. Juba I, king of Numidia, was a firm ally of Pompey and had his own reasons to oppose Caesar. Curio had previously proposed a law to annex his kingdom outright. Juba's cavalry was widely considered among the finest in the region, and he was now marching to relieve Utica.

What followed exposed Curio's inexperience. He received conflicting reports about the size of Juba's force. It was first reported that it was enormous, but then he heard that only a small advance detachment was nearby. Curio abandoned the siege, withdrew to the coast, and then advanced inland to strike what he believed was a manageable enemy.

It was a trap. The full Numidian army was waiting. At the Battle of the Bagradas, fought in the August heat on open ground, Curio's legionaries were worn down by the conditions and outmaneuvered by Juba's cavalry. The Roman force was destroyed, and Curio died fighting rather than abandoning his men. Juba executed many of the Roman prisoners, including several senators. Only a few of Caesar's soldiers made it back to

Sicily. It was the worst Caesarian defeat of the opening phase of the war, and it showed that Caesar's cause was heavily dependent on Caesar himself. His lieutenants, however capable they were in politics, were not always great in the field. The defeat strengthened Pompeian morale in Africa and secured the province as a Pompeian base for years to come.

Caesar the Dictator

Caesar returned to Rome in December 49 BCE. Marcus Aemilius Lepidus, as praetor, proposed a law appointing him dictator by constitutional procedure. The dictatorship was an ancient office. It was reserved for national emergencies, and it gave that person extraordinary authority within Rome and Italy.

He then stood for the consulship himself and was elected for 48 BCE. After eleven days, he resigned the dictatorship. He had regained his imperium legally and was now free to pursue Pompey.

Caesar spent his short dictatorship holding consular elections, restoring administrative continuity after the Senate's flight, and passing urgent legislation, including the restoration of political rights to the descendants of Sulla's proscription victims. Caesar used it for exactly that and then resigned from the office.

It is important to distinguish this brief, constitutionally grounded appointment from what came later. Caesar would be appointed dictator again in 48, 46, and 44 BCE, each time with broader powers and fewer constraints. The last appointment, in early 44 BCE, made him dictator perpetuo—dictator in perpetuity, meaning he had no time limit. It was that appointment, not the emergency measure of 49 BCE, that truly broke with republican tradition and triggered the conspiracy that killed him.

Even so, many Romans were alarmed from the start. The comparison to Sulla, who had used the same office to carry out mass proscriptions and restructure the constitution, was impossible to avoid. Plus, Caesar had spent years criticizing exactly that precedent. His response was a policy of clemency. He pardoned enemies, released prisoners, and made it clear that Sulla's bloodbath would not be repeated. He did not do this purely out of the kindness of his heart. Caesar understood that clemency—*clementia Caesaris,* as it came to be known—was sound politics. Proscriptions would have made him feared and hated. It would have driven moderates into his enemies' camp. Restraint made him appear as a restorer of order rather than a tyrant. Many senators who had fled with Pompey had done so not out of deep ideological conviction but out of fear of being caught on the wrong side. Caesar gave them a way to come back.

The political situation was stabilizing, but the military picture remained uncertain. The war was becoming increasingly expensive. Caesar had forced access to the Roman treasury before leaving for Spain, but revenues from the provinces and the spoils of Gaul could only go so far. Pompey, by contrast, had retreated to the eastern Mediterranean, where the wealthiest provinces of the Roman world lay. The East offered far greater financial resources, a stronger naval capacity, and access to the manpower of client kingdoms stretching from Greece to Syria. Pompey likely calculated that he could sustain a long war of attrition from this base, grinding Caesar down while building an army large enough to retake the west.

The Battle of Pharsalus

At this point, Caesar was at the height of his powers. He was also known for his extraordinary physical endurance. He fought in the front rank, shared the hardships of his men, and intervened personally at critical moments on the battlefield. Ancient sources suggest he suffered from some form of seizure disorder, though the nature of his condition is debated by historians. His soldiers were devoted to him, and that loyalty had been forged over years of hard campaigning.

By the summer of 48 BCE, Pompey commanded a large army in Macedonia. The senators who had fled Rome regarded themselves as the legitimate Roman government and had established a functioning political body in exile.

The anti-Caesarian position was strong. Caesar did not have enough ships to transport his full army, and it took weeks to land his forces on the Albanian coast. He then advanced on Dyrrachium (modern Durres), which was Pompey's main base in the region. It was supplied continuously from the eastern Mediterranean. Control of it meant control of Pompey's ability to sustain his army in the field. Caesar understood this. Rather than bypass it, he moved to cut it off.

What followed was one of the most unusual episodes of the war. Unable to take Dyrrachium by force, Caesar ordered his engineers to build an enormous line of fortifications encircling Pompey's position. This was one of the largest field fortification systems constructed in the ancient world. Pompey responded by building counter-walls. The two armies ended up facing each other across miles of engineered earthworks, with the smaller Caesarian force attempting to contain the larger Pompeian army. It was siege warfare in reverse.

The operations lasted months. Both sides launched raids and counter-attacks. The besieging legions suffered from supply shortages and disease. Eventually, Gallic deserters revealed an underdefended section of Caesar's lines to Pompey. The Pompeians launched a concentrated assault, broke through, and came close to routing the Caesarian force entirely. Mark Antony helped stabilize the situation, and Caesar appeared in person to steady his men. The line held, but the position was untenable. Caesar eventually withdrew, covering the retreat by leaving two legions behind to follow later.

Dyrrachium was the worst defeat of his career, but Pompey chose not to pursue. This is widely regarded as his greatest mistake of the war. Had he pressed the attack, Caesar's army might not have survived. Instead, Caesar withdrew intact into Thessaly and began looking for a chance to force a decisive engagement on his own terms.

Caesar fell back because he was short on supplies and had to forage from the local population. When the city of Gomphi refused to open its gates, he besieged and took it quickly, allowing his soldiers to plunder it as punishment. It was harsh and unusual for Caesar, but it served its purpose, as the surrounding communities submitted rather than face the same treatment.

The conservative senators with Pompey grew impatient. Pompey's strategy had always favored attrition. He had the larger force, the stronger supply lines, and the wealth of the eastern provinces behind him. Time, in theory, would work in his favor. But the senators who had followed him into exile wanted a decisive battle and to return to Rome. They pressed him relentlessly, and some questioned whether he was prolonging the war to preserve his own command. This created tension between military prudence and political legitimacy; the men who considered themselves the rightful government of Rome could not afford to look as though they were hiding from a wanted criminal. Under all of this pressure, Pompey advanced to battle Caesar.

The two armies met on the plains near Pharsalus in Thessaly in August 48 BCE. Caesar had roughly twenty-two thousand infantry. Pompey had around forty thousand to forty-five thousand, along with a massive cavalry. He had approximately seven thousand horsemen against Caesar's one thousand. The key question was whether Pompey's cavalry could sweep around Caesar's flank and collapse his line.

Caesar anticipated this, though. He quietly assembled a fourth line of seasoned infantry behind his right wing and kept them hidden. When Pompey's cavalry charged and drove Caesar's horsemen back, these infantrymen moved forward and attacked the cavalry at close quarters, targeting the riders' faces with their javelins. The tactic worked. The cavalry broke and fled, exposing Pompey's left flank. Caesar then committed his reserves, who crashed into the exposed position. Pompey's line buckled and collapsed. His men fled to the camp, but the camp fell too. Caesar's men pursued Pompey and his men until nightfall.

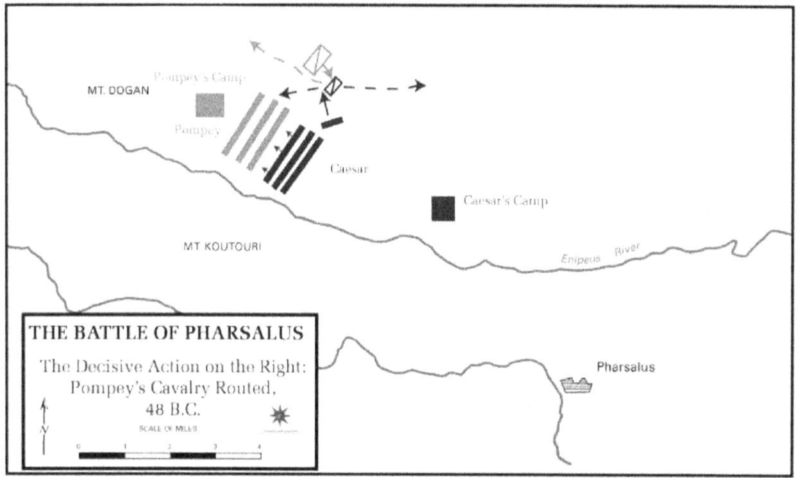

Map outlining actions of the Battle of Pharsalus. [87]

Pharsalus destroyed Pompey's field army, but it did not end the war. Still, it had fundamentally changed its character. Before Pharsalus, the conflict had been a genuine contest between two Roman commanders with comparable resources and legitimacy. After it, the Pompeian cause was reduced to scattered resistance. There were Cato and Metellus Scipio in Africa, holdouts in Spain, and Pompey himself fleeing eastward without an army. Caesar was no longer fighting a civil war between equals. He was hunting down the remnants of an opposition that had lost its military center of gravity.

In the aftermath, Caesar demonstrated his characteristic clemency toward Roman citizens who surrendered. He burned Pompey's correspondence without reading it rather than using it to identify and punish his enemies. Many senators surrendered and were pardoned, something that struck contemporaries as remarkable. The policy was politically calculated. It reduced further resistance and encouraged defections. It did not, however, end the war.

Chapter 5: Caesar and Cleopatra

War in Egypt

Pompey's destination was Egypt. It was a reasonable choice. Egypt was wealthy, its rulers owed him political debts, and it lay beyond Caesar's immediate reach. Pompey had connections there going back years. For instance, he was the one who helped restore Ptolemy XII to his throne after he had been driven out by his own people. Pompey expected gratitude. He miscalculated badly.

Egypt was ruled by the Ptolemies, a Macedonian dynasty founded by one of Alexander the Great's generals. By this point, it was effectively a client state of Rome. Ptolemy XII had borrowed enormous sums from Roman financiers to secure his restoration, leaving his successors with debts they could not repay. Now his young son, Ptolemy XIII, shared the throne (uneasily) with his sister and co-ruler Cleopatra VII. The two were at war with each other, and real power in the court sat with Ptolemy's regent, Pothinus, and the general Achillas, who, between them, dominated the young king entirely.

When Pompey's ship approached the Egyptian shore near Pelusium in September 48 BCE, he was invited to land. A small boat came out to meet him, carrying a former Roman officer now in Egyptian service. Pompey stepped in. He was stabbed to death before he reached the shore. Pothinus and his allies had decided that a Roman general on the losing side of a civil war was a liability, not an asset. Killing him was meant to demonstrate loyalty to Caesar and secure his favor.

It did not have that effect. Caesar arrived in Alexandria days later and was presented with Pompey's severed head and his signet ring. According to ancient accounts, he wept. Whether his grief was genuine is a question ancient sources raise but do not settle. Plutarch describes him as visibly shaken while leaving room for doubt about his sincerity. What is not in doubt is that Caesar understood the political problem. He had spent two years building a reputation for clemency. Being seen to profit from the murder of his greatest rival—a man who had once been his ally, his son-in-law's father, and one of Rome's most celebrated generals—would undermine everything he had worked to project. He arranged for Pompey's remains to receive proper burial rites and made it clear that the killers would face consequences.

Caesar remained in Alexandria. He had practical reasons for this. Egypt owed substantial debts to Rome stemming from the reign of Ptolemy XII, and Caesar needed money to keep his army in the field. He also announced he would decide the dispute between Ptolemy XIII and Cleopatra, citing a clause in their father's will. It was a Roman asserting Roman authority over a client kingdom, which was entirely in keeping with how Rome handled its dependencies. However, elements within the Alexandrian court resented it deeply.

Trapped in Alexander

Caesar moved into the royal palace and summoned both Ptolemy XIII and Cleopatra to present themselves before him. Ptolemy arrived, accompanied by Pothinus. Cleopatra could not. Her brother's forces controlled the city, and traveling openly to the palace would have meant almost certain death. So, she found another way. According to ancient sources, she had herself smuggled into the palace hidden inside a rolled carpet or linen sack, carried by a loyal servant past her brother's guards and into Caesar's presence.

Cleopatra was around twenty-one or twenty-two years old. Caesar was in his early fifties. She was, by all accounts, formidable. She was educated, politically astute, and fluent in multiple languages. She was notably the first ruler of her dynasty to learn Egyptian, setting her apart from all her Ptolemaic predecessors. The two became lovers.

When Ptolemy XIII discovered his sister was in the palace with Caesar, he flew into a rage and attempted to incite a riot among the Alexandrians. Caesar had him arrested. He then publicly announced that he would honor their father's will, declaring Ptolemy and Cleopatra joint rulers, which temporarily calmed the crowd.

It did not calm Pothinus. Caesar uncovered a plot between Pothinus and Achillas and had Pothinus executed. Achillas, who was already with the army outside the city, responded by marching on Alexandria. The siege had begun.

Caesar had arrived with around four thousand men, which was enough to project authority but not enough to fight a sustained urban siege. He sent urgent messages to his allies requesting relief. His survival depended on one thing: control of the harbor. He held part of the fleet and kept the sea lanes open through a combination of naval skirmishes and the tenacity of his soldiers. Without that lifeline, there was no prospect of reinforcement and no way out.

During the initial fighting around the harbor, Caesar ordered enemy ships burned to prevent their use against him. The fire spread to the waterfront. Ancient sources report that some books stored near the docks were destroyed in the blaze. Whether the great Library of Alexandria itself was damaged remains unclear, as the sources conflict with each other. What is known is that the fire at the harbor was a military decision, not a deliberate act of cultural destruction.

Bust of Cleopatra.[38]

The siege ground on. The Romans held their position but were hard-pressed by land and sea, barely keeping communications open across Alexandria's harbor. This was one of the most dangerous episodes of Caesar's career, and much of the danger was self-inflicted. He chose to entangle himself in Egypt's dynastic struggle with too few troops to control it.

Arsinoe, Cleopatra's younger sister, escaped from the palace and attached herself to the besieging army. The general Achillas was killed by her faction, and a eunuch named Ganymedes took command in his place. Arsinoe proved capable, and her presence gave the opposition renewed focus and unity. However, at some point during the siege, the Alexandrians must have grown frustrated with her leadership and petitioned Caesar to release Ptolemy XIII, offering Arsinoe in exchange.

Caesar agreed. He may have calculated that Ptolemy's presence in the rebel camp would fracture the opposition, that rival factions would turn on each other once the figurehead was among them. His officers argued against it, but Caesar overruled them. Ptolemy walked free and immediately rejoined the besieging forces. The attacks intensified. In the account later circulated under Caesar's name (it was almost certainly written by his officer Aulus Hirtius), the decision is defended, but the reasoning has not convinced many readers, ancient or modern.

The wider war was not standing still either. In Africa, the Pompeian forces under Cato and Metellus Scipio had regrouped and grown stronger in the wake of Pharsalus. In Spain, Pompeian commanders were regaining ground. In the Adriatic, a Pompeian fleet was operating freely and threatening supply lines to Italy. Caesar, the conqueror of Gaul, was pinned down in a palace in Alexandria by a conflict he had stumbled into through his own misjudgments.

Victory in Egypt

Relief came in early 47 BCE. Mithridates of Pergamum gathered a substantial force, crossed the Sinai into Egypt, and captured the key port of Pelusium. This was the breakthrough Caesar needed. Pelusium controlled the main land corridor from Syria into Egypt, and its fall forced Ptolemy XIII to divide his forces between containing Mithridates and maintaining the siege of Alexandria. Caesar was no longer isolated. He moved quickly to link up with his ally and took command of the combined force.

The decisive engagement came at the Battle of the Nile in February 47 BCE. A substantial Egyptian force, with some Pompeian elements, took up a defensive position in the Nile Delta region. Caesar was cautious about a frontal assault. The Egyptian heavy infantry was formidable, and they had a small naval force operating on the river. Control of the water determined who could move and who could not.

He chose an indirect approach instead. He sent engineers to find a suitable crossing point upstream, established a bridgehead away from the Egyptian lines, and built a pontoon bridge. His Gallic and German cavalry—veterans of the Gallic Wars now serving in his eastern force—crossed and attacked the Egyptian army from the rear. The infantry, armed with long spears, could not maneuver quickly enough to meet the threat. The Egyptian line collapsed. Ptolemy XIII fled and drowned in the

Nile while attempting to escape. Caesar returned to Alexandria. The city submitted without a fight.

Caesar remained in Egypt for several months after the victory. He had practical reasons for staying. Cleopatra's position needed to be stabilized before he could safely leave. Installing a friendly ruler on Egypt's throne was one thing, but securing her against internal opposition was another. Egypt's grain supply and finances also required attention, and Caesar needed to ensure that the kingdom's resources would flow toward Rome rather than against it. He was also positioning himself diplomatically in the East, where client kingdoms needed to understand where Roman authority now sat.

A 17th-century etching of the Battle of the Nile.[89]

During this period, Caesar traveled the Nile with Cleopatra in a display of royal spectacle. Months later, she gave birth to a son she named Ptolemy Caesar, also known as Caesarion. Cleopatra presented the child as Caesar's heir. Caesar did not legally adopt the child or name him his heir. He neither publicly claimed nor repudiated the boy.

At this stage, the succession question was not yet the explosive issue it would later become. Caesar had not designated any heir, and the political crisis around Caesarion only fully ignited after Caesar's assassination, when Octavian's position as named heir in Caesar's will made Caesarion a potential rival. Under Augustus, the existence of a living son of Caesar and Cleopatra became genuinely dangerous, and Caesarion was eventually killed on Augustus's orders. Roman aristocratic culture was deeply suspicious of Eastern monarchy, and a child born outside Roman law to an Egyptian queen had no realistic path to formal recognition as a Roman heir anyway. However, some in Rome feared the implications of the child's existence. Others denied he was Caesar's son at all.

Caesar left Egypt in the summer of 47 BCE. He had been absent from the wider war for months, and the situation had deteriorated. Mark Antony, managing affairs in Rome as Caesar's deputy, was struggling to maintain order. Italy was restive, and the Pompeian forces in Africa under Cato and Metellus Scipio had only continued to strengthen.

In 46 BCE, Cleopatra traveled to Rome with Caesarion and stayed as Caesar's guest. It was a very unpopular move. Roman aristocratic opinion was hostile to foreign monarchs at the best of times, and Cleopatra's presence and her relationship with the most powerful man in Rome alarmed many. Her position had been considerably strengthened by Caesar's support. Egypt remained within Rome's sphere of influence, but Cleopatra was no longer simply a dependent client. She had leverage, and she used it skillfully to expand Egyptian influence in the Levant. The political implications of her relationship with Caesar were not lost on anyone in Rome.

I Came, I Saw, I Conquered

One of Rome's most formidable enemies had been Mithridates VI of Pontus, who fought three wars against Rome and at one point drove Roman forces out of Asia Minor entirely. In 88 BCE, he ordered the massacre of tens of thousands of Roman and Italian citizens across Asia Minor in a single coordinated attack. This event is known as the Asiatic Vespers, and it made him the most hated enemy in the East that Rome had ever faced. He was eventually brought down not by Rome but by his own son, Pharnaces II, who led a revolt against him. Mithridates VI attempted suicide when the revolt succeeded. However, the poison failed. He was killed by a bodyguard on his own orders.

In 63 BCE, Pharnaces II became ruler of the Bosporan Kingdom, centered in what is now Crimea, which was nominally a client of Rome. The civil war gave him his opportunity. Caesar's veteran legions were committed in Egypt or preparing for the African campaign. The forces available to Rome in Asia Minor were limited, and Pharnaces knew it. With Caesar trapped in Alexandria and no credible Roman army nearby to oppose him, Pharnaces II recruited a large force and moved into Armenia and Cappadocia, seizing territory including cities under direct Roman control. Ancient sources accuse him of harsh reprisals against the populations he conquered, including the mutilation of prisoners.

Caesar, who was still in Egypt, ordered Gnaeus Domitius Calvinus to take command of Roman forces in Asia Minor and deal with the threat. Calvinus gathered what troops he could, supplemented by forces from local rulers who had their own reasons to oppose Pharnaces.

It was not enough. The Romans were defeated at the Battle of Nicopolis in 48 BCE. Calvinus managed to get his legion off the field, but Pharnaces was now free to range through northern Asia Minor largely unchecked. His advance was only halted when his deputy in Crimea revolted, forcing him to return east and suppress the rebellion.

Pharnaces dealt with the revolt quickly and returned to Armenia in 47 BCE, confident he could consolidate his gains before Caesar could respond. He miscalculated. Caesar marched with extraordinary speed from Egypt through Syria and into Asia Minor, assembling legions and allied detachments as he went. Pharnaces attempted to buy time. He offered bribes and even proposed a marriage alliance. Caesar negotiated while preparing for battle. He advanced to high ground near Zela in what is now northern Turkey. His men began constructing their usual fortified camp on the elevated position.

Before they could finish, Pharnaces ordered his army to attack uphill. It was a bold and unconventional decision. Some historians believe he wanted to catch the Romans while they were still unprepared and in disorder. Pharnaces deployed scythed chariots at the front of the assault. The chariots initially caused disruption, but the disciplined Roman infantry used their javelins to bring down the drivers and neutralize the threat. The attack stalled.

Caesar's legionaries then pushed downhill into the Bosporan force and routed it. The engagement was short and permanently ended the threat. According to ancient accounts, the victory was achieved with relatively light casualties on the Roman side, though such figures should always be treated with caution.

It was after Zela that Caesar reportedly uttered the phrase, "Veni, vidi, vici"—"I came, I saw, I conquered." The line was preserved by Suetonius. After Pharnaces died, Caesar recognized Mithridates of Pergamum with territory in the region.

The situation in Italy had deteriorated while Caesar was on campaign. Mark Antony was managing affairs as Caesar's deputy, with Lepidus holding authority in Rome itself. The debt crisis had been building throughout the civil war. Years of disruption and uncertainty had strained

Italy's economy, and now the tension erupted into street violence. Antony moved to suppress it but was delayed by a mutiny among some of Caesar's legions. Clashes broke out in the Forum between his men and those of Publius Cornelius Dolabella, a political opponent.

By the time Caesar landed in Italy, he found a city in disorder. He moved quickly. He relieved Antony of his responsibilities–Antony was a capable soldier but had proven an unreliable administrator–and turned his attention to the mutinous troops.

Caesar's handling of the mutiny became one of the most celebrated episodes of his career. He assembled the men, addressed them as "civilians," and dismissed them from service. The word "civilian" was a calculated insult. For Roman soldiers, whose sense of honor and identity were inseparable from their status as legionaries, it struck at the core of who they were. The men broke. They begged to be readmitted and handed over the ringleaders themselves. Caesar accepted them back after a deliberate show of hesitation. The mutiny collapsed. Caesar also moved to defuse the debt agitation politically, finding offices for some of those involved, including Dolabella. Rome had been pacified.

Caesar had little time to consolidate his gains. The Pompeians (which we call Republicans moving onward) in Africa had formalized their alliance with King Juba of Numidia and assembled a substantial force. In Spain, Caesar's governor had been overthrown, and the Republicans had regained control of the provinces, which led to more manpower and valuable mines. Caesar placed Lepidus in charge of Italy, raised new funds, assembled a large army, and sailed for Africa in 46 BCE. It was the more immediate threat, and he intended to deal with it first.

Chapter 6: Final Campaigns and Return to Rome

The Bloodshed Continues

Caesar landed in Africa in December 47 BCE with an advance force, waiting for the bulk of his army to cross from Italy. He eventually assembled roughly thirty thousand men, but in the early weeks, he was operating with far fewer men, and he was in a vulnerable position. The Republicans harassed him while he waited for reinforcements.

Ancient sources report that Caesar elevated a minor member of the Scipio family to his staff during this period, possibly to counter a widespread belief among ordinary soldiers that no Scipio could be defeated in Africa. This superstition was rooted in the memory of Scipio Africanus and the Second Punic War. This may have been deliberate propaganda or just a way to boost morale.

The Republican force was formidable. It was commanded by Quintus Caecilius Metellus Pius Scipio, with Titus Labienus, once one of Caesar's finest lieutenants in the Gallic campaigns, directing their army in the field. Their alliance with Juba of Numidia gave them a large force of elite Numidian cavalry, which would prove to be a persistent problem for Caesar's infantry-heavy army.

Caesar had secured an alliance with the Kingdom of Mauretania, whose forces raided Numidia and prevented Juba from committing his full strength against the Caesarians. Republican supply lines to Rome were not secure either. A small Republican naval force was operating in the central

Mediterranean, which threatened Caesar's own communications. The Republican command structure was also divided among several leaders, which may have complicated coordination. Cato the Younger was present in Africa and exerted strong political influence within the leadership. It was, to put it lightly, an uneasy coalition.

Caesar's full force did not assemble until January 46 BCE. In the meantime, he moved against local towns to secure his position and gather supplies. Once, after taking a small settlement, his force was returning to their base at Ruspina (in modern Tunisia) when Labienus appeared with a largely cavalry-based army and moved to surround them. Caesar's men were mostly heavy infantry. These were battle-hardened and disciplined men, but they lacked the mobility to simply outrun encirclement. Caesar extended his lines to prevent being outflanked. Labienus, who knew Caesar's tactics very well, extended his own lines to take advantage of his numerical superiority. The Numidian horsemen began circling and throwing javelins into the Roman formation. It was starting to look like this would not end well for Caesar.

However, Caesar kept his nerve. Later sources claim he personally intervened when an eagle standard bearer began to fall back, seizing the standard himself and turning it to face the enemy, though this account is likely an embellishment. What is clear is that the Caesarian line held. Caesar ordered his men to charge forward and throw their javelins as they closed in on the enemy. The sudden aggression disrupted Labienus's formation and created enough chaos for Caesar to disengage. He withdrew his force to Ruspina and fortified the camp.

This engagement was not a victory. It was at best a successful withdrawal after near-encirclement, and it exposed how vulnerable Caesar's force was until his full army arrived.

Bust of middle-aged Julius Caesar.[40]

Victory in Africa

Thankfully for Caesar, the Republican commanders adopted a cautious strategy that bought him the time he needed. They had good reasons to avoid immediate battle. Their Numidian cavalry gave them a significant advantage in open country, and they believed that Caesar's supplies would deteriorate the longer the campaign dragged on. A weakened Caesar, they hoped, would be easier to destroy or force into surrender.

Political pressure within the Republican leadership complicated this. Cato the Younger, for instance, pushed for more aggressive action, arguing that delay helped Caesar more than it helped them. Eventually, the Republicans moved toward a more offensive posture. It gave Caesar the battle he had been waiting for.

The African campaign is documented primarily in the *De Bello Africo*, which is part of the Caesarian body of writings, although it was almost certainly not written by Caesar himself. The author remains unknown. It is a valuable source, though like all ancient military accounts, it should be read with caution.

The two armies met at Thapsus on what most sources place in April 46 BCE, though some scholars give a February date due to calendar conversion issues between the Julian and older Roman calendars. The battlefield was a narrow corridor of low-lying ground with the sea on one side and a lake and marsh on the other. This terrain neutralized much of the Republican cavalry advantage by removing the open ground Numidian horsemen needed to encircle and harass an enemy force–the same tactic that had nearly destroyed Caesar at Ruspina.

Caesar had anticipated the Republicans' reliance on war elephants and drilled his men specifically in how to counter them. He placed his most experienced legions in the positions most likely to face the elephants and stationed his archers and slingers to target them. When the battle began, he ordered the missile troops forward against the animals. The elephants panicked and stampeded back into the Republican lines, causing chaos. Caesar's cavalry then moved against the enemy camp. The besieged garrison at Thapsus made a sortie but was driven back. Metellus Scipio could not hold his formation together as the left wing began to break. Juba's forces abandoned the field once it was clear the Republicans would be defeated.

What followed the battle was ugly. Caesar's soldiers massacred large numbers of prisoners. Ancient sources report that Caesar ordered them to stop, but he could not get them to listen.

The Battle of Thapsus destroyed the main Republican army in Africa. Metellus Scipio fled but did not escape; he was cornered at sea and killed himself rather than surrender. Juba and Marcus Petreius were trapped and chose death on their own terms, fighting a duel whose outcome ancient sources describe differently, with the survivor killed by a slave. Cato the Younger, the political backbone of the Republican cause, retreated to Utica and took his own life rather than accept Caesar's mercy.

With their army destroyed and their leading figures dead or dying, organized Republican resistance had effectively collapsed. Spain was still an issue, as Republican commanders still held significant territory and manpower there. But the war's center of gravity had shifted decisively. Caesar had broken the Republican cause in Africa.

Forces under Publius Sittius, operating alongside Caesar's Mauretanian allies, defeated elements of Juba's army and cut off escape routes. Caesar moved through the province imposing financial penalties on communities and individuals who had supported his enemies. Roman commanders financed their campaigns through a combination of state resources, booty, loans, and confiscation, and Caesar needed funds to pay his army and to consolidate his political position. He then annexed part of Numidia, turning it into the new province of Africa Nova, and granted territory to his Mauretanian allies.

Ancient sources, including Suetonius, report a rumor that Caesar had an affair with Eunoë, the wife of the Mauretanian king Bogud. This ancient rumor is impossible to verify, but it surely didn't help Caesar's reputation as a womanizer.

To Italy!

Once Caesar had arranged affairs to his satisfaction in Africa, he returned to Rome. He was greeted by supporters and sycophants eager for his favor.

Caesar increasingly controlled the electoral process, often directly appointing magistrates rather than leaving elections to run their traditional course. Those who had opposed him, such as Cicero, appeared publicly accepting of his rule. In private letters, Cicero lamented the loss of Republican liberty.

The Roman public cheered, though. In September 46 BCE, Caesar celebrated four triumphs: one for Gaul, one for Egypt, one for Pontus, and one for Africa. The triumph was a ritual through which the Senate formally recognized a commander's victory and paraded his conquests before the Roman people. Caesar now turned that Republican institution to his own purposes. All of his major campaigns had involved the defeat of Roman citizens as well as foreign enemies, but the triumphs presented only foreign victories. The Gauls, Egyptians, Pontic forces, and Africans were the enemies on display. The civil war was quietly set aside. It was a careful piece of political theater that recast one man's seizure of power as the expansion of Rome. Each triumph reinforced the image of Caesar not merely as victor in a civil war but as conqueror of the world. Caesar wanted to normalize something that the Roman Republic had no precedent for—a single man who had defeated everyone.

The constitutional reality was also unprecedented. In 46 BCE, Caesar was appointed dictator for ten years, under the title dictator rei publicae constituendae (dictator for the purpose of settling the constitution), the same title Sulla had used. He also held the consulship repeatedly and earned a range of other honors and powers that collectively placed him beyond any check of the Republican system. In public after 46 BCE, he was attended by seventy-two lictors (a bodyguard)—twenty-four for each dictatorship he held simultaneously. A consul would normally receive twelve lictors. Caesar had symbols too. A golden chair, a purple robe, and a statue placed among those of the kings of Rome all helped to build his image. He could defend why he earned each honor, but this power grab was becoming alarming. Elite resentment grew quietly, and conspiratorial networks began to form.

Cleopatra visited Rome again during this period, staying at Caesar's villa across the Tiber with Ptolemy XIV. Cicero, who visited her there, found her arrogant. On September 26th, 46 BCE, the final day of his triumph, Caesar dedicated the Temple of Venus Genetrix in his new Forum. Inside stood a golden statue of Cleopatra. It was a striking gesture, as Cleopatra was both foreign and still alive. It seemed as if Caesar was associating the mother of his child with the divine ancestry of his own family line.

Caesar did not divorce Calpurnia despite having no children with her and despite his affair with Cleopatra. Her family was powerful and well connected. Whether he genuinely respected and loved her is impossible to know. Roman elite men were not expected to be sexually faithful in the modern sense, and Caesar's affairs were notorious enough to feature in his soldiers' marching songs.

Caesar also began to show particular favor to his grand-nephew Octavian, grandson of his beloved sister. Octavian had already been in Caesar's orbit for some time. He saw something in the young man that others, put off by his slight build and fragile health, apparently missed.

A bust of Caesarion.[41]

Caesar's Last Battles

The civil war was not over. The sons of Pompey the Great, Gnaeus and Sextus, had assumed leadership of the Republican cause and seized control of most of Roman Iberia, exploiting the incompetence and greed of the governor Caesar had appointed there. Labienus, who had survived Thapsus, joined them and used his considerable military talent to assemble a large force. Ancient sources claim there were up to thirteen legions, though many were newly raised rather than veteran formations.

Pompey the Great had commanded in Spain for years and built deep networks of loyalty among local elites, veteran soldiers, and provincial communities. Those ties had passed to his sons. The peninsula had strong recruitment potential, experienced local fighters who had absorbed Roman military discipline, and enormous resources in mining wealth. It was also geographically distant from Rome, which meant it would be difficult to reinforce quickly and easy to hold against a cautious enemy.

Caesar had suppressed Spain in 49 BCE, but Pompeian roots ran deeper there than a single campaign could destroy. If Gnaeus and Sextus could consolidate their position, they would control the western half of the Roman world. The situation was serious enough that Caesar left Italy in November 46 BCE with limited forces that would be reinforced by additional legions upon their arrival. He made the journey to Spain with extraordinary speed, impressing his contemporaries.

Caesar summoned his grand-nephew Octavian to join him during the campaign, an early sign of his favor. However, Octavian did not reach him due to illness.

Caesar began operations in southern Spain in early 45 BCE. He relieved the Republican siege of Ulia and moved on Córdoba, one of the most important cities in the peninsula. The fighting was brutal. Both sides committed atrocities and gave little quarter.

Gnaeus, following Labienus's counsel, refused to be drawn into open battle. He shadowed Caesar's legions through the winter, believing that Caesar's army would be worn down by cold, disease, and supply problems. Caesar responded by moving suddenly on Ategua and besieging it. The Republican commander executed deserters, but the city fell in February 45 BCE.

The fall of Ategua unsettled Gnaeus. His own men were growing restive, and desertions were increasing. He could no longer delay. His larger army was struggling to supply itself, and the initiative had shifted.

There was further maneuvering near the River Salsum, which was indecisive. Eventually, both armies finally met on the plain near Munda in southern Spain. What made Munda dangerous for Caesar was not just the terrain or the numbers. Many of his most experienced veterans had retired after years of service. His legions were understrength. The Republican forces included hardened Spanish fighters who had absorbed local combat styles and were fighting on familiar ground. The Republicans held a strong elevated position, and Caesar, outnumbered and attacking uphill, was in a situation that his own tactical principles would have normally argued against.

The battle that followed was unlike anything else in the civil war. Ancient sources describe hours of grinding, inconclusive infantry combat, with both sides holding their ground and neither breaking. At some point, Caesar personally entered the fighting and rallied Legio X on the right flank. Later accounts describe him leading from the front to prevent a collapse, though some of the details may be embellishment. According to Appian, Caesar later said that at previous battles he had fought for victory, but at Munda, he had fought for his life. It was the closest he had come to personal defeat since Dyrrachium.

The breakthrough came when Gnaeus shifted a legion to reinforce his left, weakening his flank in doing so. The Mauretanian cavalry exploited the opening and struck the exposed position. Combined with the pressure of the sustained infantry assault, the Republican line finally gave way. Once it broke, the rout was total. Ancient sources claim around thirty thousand Republican casualties, though this figure sounds inflated and should be treated with caution. Labienus died on the field. Gnaeus fled with what remained of his forces, but he was captured and killed shortly afterward near Lauro.

Sextus Pompeius escaped. He would go on to control Sicily, disrupt the grain supply to Rome, and challenge the Second Triumvirate for years. He would not be fully suppressed until 36 BCE. So, while Munda ended organized Republican resistance on land, it did not end the civil war.

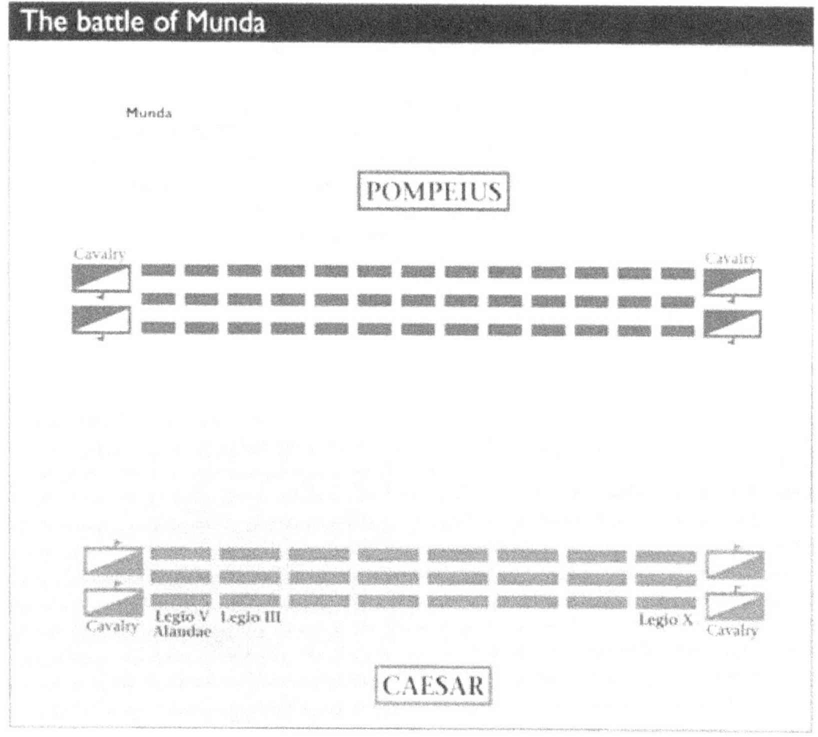

Initial deployment of armies at the Battle of Munda.[42]

Chapter 7: Caesar's Dictatorship and Reforms

Remaking Rome

Munda had ended the military threat. Caesar returned to Rome through southern Gaul, establishing veterans' colonies along the way. He also reconciled with Mark Antony, whom he would later name co-consul. He appointed Brutus as praetor for 44 BCE, a deliberate gesture of inclusion toward someone who had come over from the Republican side.

Back in Rome, he celebrated a triumph for the Spanish campaign. It was controversial. Triumphs traditionally celebrated victories over foreign enemies. This one celebrated the killing of fellow Romans, and many found it distasteful, including men Caesar had pardoned, among them Cicero and Brutus.

The forms of Republican government still existed. The Senate still met. Elections still took place. However, the reality was something else entirely. Caesar had packed the Senate with allies, controlled the electoral process, and commanded an army loyal to him personally rather than to the state. The institutions of the Roman Republic functioned as instruments of his will.

Many senators hated it. They believed that only the Roman Republic could guarantee their freedom and that one all-powerful man—however capable—reduced them to subjects. To men like Cicero, the parallel with the Greek tyrants was obvious. But the most dangerous opponents were not the ones who complained openly. Brutus and Cassius had been pardoned and given offices. They said little, but they were watching for a chance to act.

The honors had accumulated steadily since Pharsalus in 48 BCE. The Senate granted Caesar the title praefectus moribus (prefect of morals), giving him the right to revise the senatorial rolls and fill them with his own men. He was given the power to declare war and make peace, which had traditionally belonged to the popular assemblies. Each victory brought more honors. The Senate granted them eagerly, partly out of loyalty, partly out of fear, and partly because men who wanted his favor understood that honors cost them nothing.

By early 44 BCE, the accumulation of honors had reached its endpoint. Caesar was appointed dictator perpetuo (dictator in perpetuity). There was no time limit for this office and no expectation of resignation. It was a formal break with everything the dictatorship had meant. His first dictatorship in 49 BCE had been brief and constitutionally irregular, though it was formally approved. After that, he held the office three more times. In 46 BCE, he secured it for ten years. Not even during the Second Punic War, when Hannibal was marching through Italy, had the dictatorship been extended to anything like that length.

Caesar the King?

Even those sympathetic to Caesar likely had doubts about his growing power. He wore distinctive purple and triumphal dress on occasions that would previously have been reserved for specific ceremonies. What alarmed observers was not the color itself—Roman magistrates had always used purple in various forms. But Caesar wore it often, and he seemed to have claimed it as his. He sat on a gilded chair. He had his portrait stamped on coins, a practice unknown in Rome but standard among the Hellenistic monarchies of the East.

A denarius of Julius Caesar.[43]

The question of whether Caesar wanted to be king was tested publicly in February 44 BCE at the festival of Lupercalia. Mark Antony, who was participating in the festival, approached Caesar as he sat watching from the Rostra (a large, elevated platform in the Roman Forum) and placed a diadem on his head, saying the people offered it to him. A few in the crowd applauded. Most were silent. Caesar removed it. Antony offered it again. When Caesar set it aside as an offering to Jupiter and declared that Jupiter alone was king of the Romans, the crowd cheered loudly.

Whether the episode was staged or a genuine offer, it revealed that the Roman people were not ready for a king, and Caesar knew it. Earlier that same year, tribunes Marullus and Flavus had removed royal insignia that had been placed on Caesar's statues in the Forum. Caesar had them stripped of their office and expelled from the Senate. As tribunes, they were the traditional defenders of the common people. Punishing them for defending Republican symbols turned public sentiment against him. Some sources report that when members of a crowd greeted him as rex ("king") on the Appian Way, Caesar replied, "I am not Rex, but Caesar," deflecting the title while doing nothing to dismiss the suspicion behind it.

His accumulation of powers resembled those of a monarch, whether or not he intended to assume the title. Some contemporaries, including Suetonius and Plutarch, portrayed him as increasingly arrogant after his victories. He remained seated when the Senate approached him in formal delegations, surrounded himself with flatterers, and was less willing to read public sentiment than he had earlier in his career. Whether this reflects reality or the bias of sources writing after his death is difficult to say. What is clear is that he antagonized even some of his supporters, men who felt they were his equals and believed they had not received their share of the honors. In Rome, politics was very personal. Dignitas (reputation and the respect of one's peers) was the currency of public life. Caesar's behavior implied that his own stood so far above everyone else's that theirs barely registered.

Open opposition was limited, but there were reasons for this beyond just cowardice. Many senators had died in the civil war. Some aristocratic families had been politically weakened. Many of those who remained owed their positions directly to Caesar; they had been appointed, promoted, or pardoned by him. Refusing to grant him honors would have appeared disloyal in a political culture that rewarded loyalty. To put it simply, the Senate did not just cave. It had to operate within a system Caesar had changed so thoroughly that independent action carried serious risk.

The Senate renamed the month of Quintilis—the month of Caesar's birth—Julius, a name that has endured in the Western calendar for over two millennia. He had already dedicated the Temple of Venus Genetrix, tying his family's claimed descent from Venus to a permanent religious monument at the center of Roman public life. The Julian line traced its ancestry from Venus through Aeneas to his son Iulus. This was not unusual; claims of divine ancestry were common among Roman elites, and they were politically useful, though they were not necessarily taken as literal theology. What made Caesar's use of it different was the scale and the context. Hellenistic monarchs routinely emphasized divine lineage to legitimize their rule. By building a temple, placing Cleopatra's statue inside it, and publicly associating his own family with divine origin, Caesar was using the language of an Eastern monarchy in the heart of the Roman Republic. His opponents noticed.

His veterans remained fiercely loyal. The urban population was more divided. Many still revered him as the man who had ended the civil wars and delivered bread and entertainment, but some sources suggest there was unease among segments of the populace about his concentration of power. After his assassination, Antony's funeral oration unleashed popular fury against the conspirators. The city erupted in violence, and the assassins were driven from Rome. That reaction suggests Caesar still had deep popular support. The conspiracy came not from the streets but from the Senate and from men he had trusted.

The Reforms of Caesar

Caesar was a great general, a gifted writer, and an ambitious reformer. Like Sulla before him, he wanted to end the political instability that had plagued Rome for decades. Throughout his years in power, his reforms touched many areas of Roman political and social life.

Citizenship Reform

Caesar carried out a census prompted by concerns about the decline in the citizen population after years of civil war. Many inhabitants had been claiming the grain dole (grain given to citizens each month for free) when they didn't need it, so he reformed the distribution to ensure it reached those with a legitimate right to it. He imposed limits on prolonged absences from the provinces for senators and members of the elite. He extended citizenship to eligible inhabitants of Gaul and Hispania, rewarding allies and facilitating the integration of those provinces into Roman political structures. Only a small portion of the population gained citizenship through these measures, though; it was predominantly the local elite who entered the citizenry. He also granted citizenship to skilled immigrants, such as doctors, who settled in Italy.

Debt was a serious problem. Years of civil war had left many poorer citizens unable to meet their obligations, and the resulting tensions fed the factionalism that had long destabilized the city. Caesar restructured debt repayment by deducting previously paid interest from the principal owed and by allowing property to be valued at pre-war rates rather than the deflated values produced by the conflict. He also introduced limits on interest rates. These measures protected debtors without simply wiping out what creditors were owed.

Infrastructure Projects

Caesar was a builder on a large scale. His infrastructure projects served two purposes. It would help the urban poor by stimulating the economy. These projects would also serve as a visible legitimization of his rule. He ordered roads built across Italy, often at his own expense. He expanded the Roman Forum by constructing the Forum Iulium (Forum of Caesar). The Temple of Venus Genetrix stood at its center. He improved drainage and urban planning in Rome and undertook several other development projects.

He also ordered the refounding of Carthage and Corinth—both of which had been destroyed by Rome in the previous century—and resettled large numbers of the urban poor in these new colonies. Both became important urban centers in the Roman world.

These projects were funded through war spoils, state revenues, and taxes from the provinces. That is the other side of Roman development. The wealth that built the roads and forums was often extracted from the provinces, sometimes at considerable cost to the people who lived there. The provinces benefited from Roman infrastructure and stability over time, but the relationship was rarely equal.

Forum of Julius Caesar and Temple of Venus Genitrix.[44]

Reorganization of Government

Caesar's political reforms strengthened his grip on power while also addressing genuine administrative needs. He expanded the Senate from roughly six hundred to perhaps as many as nine hundred members. This provided more magistrates and commanders for a growing empire, but it also packed the Senate with his supporters. He increased the number of quaestors, aediles, and praetors to ensure the administration ran smoothly. Plus, he could use these offices to reward loyal men. He restricted political collegia, the street-level associations that had long been a source of factional violence in Rome. He reorganized the courts and restructured jury pools. Even his opponents acknowledged that he was fair in his legal decisions.

Caesar transformed the dictatorship from a temporary emergency office into a long-term governing position. He made the Urban Prefect and Master of Horse into important administrative roles, giving them authority over Rome and Italy that had previously rested with the Senate. By 44 BCE, he had forced the Senate to grant him the right to designate magistrates for years when he would be absent from the city.

The traditional elite found itself increasingly sidelined. Caesar would occasionally grant brief consulships to supporters, bending convention to reward loyalty. This alarmed many in Rome. Change had always been associated with instability, and Caesar was generating a great deal of it.

Military Reforms

Caesar had watched Pompey's veterans destabilize Roman politics through their demands for land. He avoided the same problem by settling his veterans in colonies outside Italy, namely in Africa, Spain, and Gaul. These settlements helped consolidate Roman control in the provinces and, over time, became important centers of Roman culture in those regions. They were settlements, not standing garrisons, though veterans provided experienced manpower in times of crisis.

Caesar also broadened recruitment. He had always been quick to raise auxiliary units—Gallic and German cavalry in particular—and he increasingly enlisted provincials alongside Romans. This was not a fully systematic reform, but it pointed toward what the imperial army would later become. He promised his soldiers land and substantial rewards, and his generosity to his men was key to the loyalty they showed him throughout his campaigns.

Reform of the Calendar

Caesar remained Pontifex Maximus throughout his dictatorship. The College of Pontiffs was responsible for maintaining the calendar, but years of neglect had left it badly out of alignment with the solar year. Festivals were no longer held at the right time of year. Caesar decided to replace the old lunar calendar with a solar one. He based the reform on the work of Sosigenes, an Alexandrian astronomer, drawing on Egyptian and Hellenistic astronomical calculations that had long established the solar year at 365 and a quarter days. The new Julian calendar introduced a regular year of 365 days and a leap year of 366 days every four years to account for the quarter-day remainder.

To realign the calendar before the new system could begin, Caesar ordained that 46 BCE would last 445 days. The Romans called it the year of confusion. The Julian calendar took effect on January 1st, 45 BCE, and became the official system in the Roman administration. Local calendars lasted in some provinces for cultural reasons, but the Julian calendar quickly replaced the old Roman system. It remained the standard in the Western world for over fifteen centuries.

After returning from the civil wars, Caesar showed little sign of slowing down. He enjoyed himself. He had affairs, drank, and lived like a wealthy Roman aristocrat. But he also worked constantly.

His behavior became increasingly high-handed. Those who disagreed with him grew cautious about saying so. Caesar had lived through decades of political violence and had survived too much to think he was still vulnerable. That belief may have cost him his life.

Chapter 8: Assassination and Aftermath

Growing Dangers

By 44 BCE, Caesar faced no open military opposition, though political resentment remained among some of the elite. He was busy implementing reforms and preparing for new campaigns. Several ancient sources portray him as increasingly dismissive of senatorial protocol and less attentive to the political mood than he had been earlier in his career.

A small group of senators began to conspire against him. Cassius Longinus, an able soldier and politician, was one of the instigators. He was alarmed by Caesar's accumulation of power and believed action was necessary before Caesar left Rome on campaign. Caesar was preparing a large-scale Eastern campaign, first against the Dacians north of the Danube, then against the Parthian Empire. The Parthian campaign, in particular, was very ambitious. It was widely seen as an attempt to avenge the catastrophic Roman defeat at Carrhae in 53 BCE, where Crassus and his army had been destroyed. Caesar planned a multi-year expedition that would take him deep into the East. Rome would be left under the control of his deputies, men like Antony and Lepidus, for an indefinite period. For the conspirators, this was the closing of a window. Once Caesar left, the opportunity to act would be gone for years, and his lieutenants would tighten their grip on the city in his absence.

Cassius recruited his brother-in-law, Marcus Brutus. Brutus was a man of principle who had fought with Pompey against Caesar because he was a Republican, even though Pompey had murdered his father. Caesar had pardoned him after the Battle of Pharsalus and shown him considerable favor. Rumor was that Brutus was Caesar's illegitimate son, though this is unverifiable. He was also said to be descended from the Brutus who had expelled the kings of Rome centuries earlier. This lineage must have weighed heavily on him. He joined the conspiracy despite his personal connection to Caesar, apparently convinced that the Roman Republic needed Caesar to be gone.

The conspirators recruited carefully. Eventually, more than sixty senators were involved. Not all of them were ideological Republicans acting on principle. Some had personal grievances. These were men who felt passed over for honors, sidelined by Caesar's patronage networks, or humiliated by his dominance. Cassius himself was driven partly by genuine Republican conviction and partly by wounded pride.

The mix of motives made the group politically disunited. They had a plan to kill Caesar, but they had no plan for what came after. There was no agreement on how to restore the Roman Republic, no strategy for dealing with Caesar's veterans, and no preparation for the Roman people's reaction.

They debated whether to kill Mark Antony alongside Caesar. Brutus argued against it. Killing only Caesar would make the act look like tyrannicide rather than a coup, which might prevent a new civil war. The others accepted this reluctantly. It proved to be a serious miscalculation. Since Antony survived, he controlled Caesar's papers and funds, and within days, he had turned the city against them.

By March 44 BCE, the conspirators knew they had to move. The Senate meeting of March 15th—the Ides of March, just a normal day in the Roman calendar that would become famous—was their opportunity. Caesar had no formal bodyguard. He was normally surrounded by friends and clients, but in the Senate, he was much more accessible.

At least one ancient source records that a soothsayer warned him his life was in danger on the Ides of March. Caesar is said to have ignored the warning. He may have known conspiracies were being discussed but doubted anyone would act. He had survived so much. He probably believed he was untouchable.

The Most Famous Assassination in History

The Senate was to meet in the Curia of Pompey within the Theatre of Pompey complex. The traditional Senate house had been destroyed in 52 BCE and was still being rebuilt. Caesar was delayed. His wife Calpurnia had dreamed of his bloodied corpse and begged him not to go. He initially agreed to cancel. Then, Decimus Brutus, one of the conspirators, arrived at the house and persuaded him otherwise, arguing it would look weak to stay home because of a bad dream. Caesar finally relented.

On his way to the Theatre of Pompey, he passed the soothsayer who had supposedly warned him about the Ides of March. According to later sources, Caesar remarked that the Ides of March had come. The soothsayer replied that they had not yet passed. Caesar went to the Senate meeting anyway.

He entered without a bodyguard—he had dismissed his Spanish guard months earlier—which made him vulnerable once inside the chamber. One of the conspirators detained Mark Antony outside, as the conspirators were aware of his formidable reputation as a soldier. Inside, roughly two hundred senators were present for what appeared to be a routine formal meeting. Around sixty of them were conspirators.

Caesar took his seat. The assassins positioned themselves around him under the pretense of joining a group petition. It was carefully staged. Lucius Tillius Cimber stepped forward first, drawing Caesar's attention with a request. Cimber then seized Caesar's toga, which was the prearranged signal for the attack. It was also a way to restrain him.

Casca struck first, stabbing Caesar in the neck. The wound was not immediately fatal. Caesar grabbed Casca's arm. According to Plutarch, he cried out, "Casca, you villain, what are you doing?" He tried to fight back, but the rest closed in. The conspirators attacked him with concealed daggers. He was stabbed twenty-three times. Some ancient sources claim that when Caesar saw Brutus among the attackers, he said in Greek, "Kai su, teknon?" ("You too, child?"). Others report he said nothing. The line "Et tu, Brute?" ("And you, Brutus?") is Shakespeare's invention. It has no basis in the ancient sources.

Caesar wrapped his toga around himself as he fell. He died at the base of a statue of Pompey, the man he had defeated in the civil war, whose cause many of the conspirators had once supported. That the most powerful man in the Roman world fell at the feet of his greatest rival, in a building that bore his rival's name, was not lost on contemporaries. The divisions of the Roman Republic had never really been resolved. They had simply been suppressed.

A later medical examination, attributed to a physician named Antistius, concluded that only one of the twenty-three wounds had been fatal.

Caesar's body reportedly lay unattended for some time before slaves finally removed it. One of the most consequential figures in the history of the ancient world died on the floor of a meeting room, surrounded by men he had pardoned.

The assassination of Caesar, a painting dated to the late 19th century. [45]

The Aftermath of the Assassination

After the assassination, the conspirators marched through Rome proclaiming that the people were free. The response was not what they had hoped for. The city did not rise to join them. The Romans had lived through decades of political violence and civil war. Most stayed off the streets. The conspirators withdrew to the Capitoline Hill when popular support failed to appear.

In the days that followed, civil war was not yet inevitable. Mark Antony negotiated a compromise in the Senate that temporarily held the city together. The assassins were granted amnesty. At the same time, Caesar's acts, appointments, and legislation were ratified and allowed to stand. It was a careful political balance. The conspirators escaped punishment, but everything Caesar had built remained in place. The arrangement suited Antony. It gave him legal continuity over Caesar's affairs while leaving the conspirators without a clear path to dismantling his legacy. For a brief moment, an uneasy peace held.

But it did not last. Caesar's funeral destroyed it. Antony delivered the eulogy and used the occasion to promote his own agenda. He displayed Caesar's bloodstained toga to the crowd, holding it up so the wounds were visible. According to some ancient sources, a wax effigy showing Caesar's twenty-three wounds was on display. Antony read the will aloud, including Caesar's gifts to the Roman people and the gardens he left for public use.

The crowd's grief turned to fury. The body was burned spontaneously in the Forum, the crowd feeding the pyre with whatever came to hand. Rioters attacked the houses of the conspirators. The city that had stood back in cautious silence days earlier had turned. The assassins had badly misjudged how deeply Caesar was beloved in the city.

Octavian, Caesar's eighteen-year-old great-nephew, was not in Rome at the time of the assassination. He was in Apollonia on the Adriatic coast, preparing to join Caesar's Parthian campaign. Once Caesar's will was read, his status as adopted heir became known quickly. Leading figures in the city took note. Antony, who was serving as consul at the time of Caesar's death, had emerged as the dominant Caesarian in Rome. He controlled Caesar's papers and funds. However, Octavian's claim to Caesar's name and legacy would prove more powerful than Antony anticipated.

Antony, as executor of Caesar's will, withheld much of Caesar's inheritance from Octavian. Octavian did not accept this quietly. He was young and had a reputation for poor health, but he was intelligent, patient, and utterly ruthless. He borrowed heavily to honor Caesar's favors to the Roman people out of his own funds, which earned him a lot of goodwill among Caesar's veterans and the urban poor. He flattered Cicero, who hoped to use him as a tool against Antony, and cultivated allies among the senators who had stayed out of the conspiracy.

Antony, meanwhile, overreached. He moved to seize the province of Cisalpine Gaul, which the conspirator Decimus Brutus was holding. The Senate declared this illegal and dispatched the two consuls of 43 BCE, Aulus Hirtius and Gaius Vibius Pansa, along with Octavian and his legions of Caesar's veterans, to oppose him. At the Battle of Mutina in 43 BCE, Antony was defeated. Both consuls died in the fighting. Ancient sources noted the convenience of their deaths, though no firm evidence of foul play exists. Octavian found himself in command of the Senate's forces, as well as his own.

He did not use that position to serve the Senate. He turned his army around and made peace with Antony. He understood that the Senate regarded him as a useful instrument, not a partner, and that Caesar's enemies were his enemies too. Together with Antony and the veteran Caesarian Lepidus, Octavian formed the Second Triumvirate in 43 BCE. Unlike the informal alliance between Caesar, Pompey, and Crassus a generation earlier, this was a legally constituted arrangement. The Lex Titia formally granted the three men extraordinary powers for five years. They had the power to make laws, appoint magistrates, and govern the Roman world between them. It was as if the Roman Republic's constitution had been suspended.

The proscriptions that followed were savage and systematic. Ancient sources give varying figures, but around three hundred senators and two thousand equestrians were targeted. The proscriptions served two purposes—political and financial. Enemies were eliminated. Their confiscated property and estates funded the triumvirs' armies. Lists of names were posted publicly. Men were dragged from their homes and killed in the street, in their gardens, and in temples where they sought refuge. Slaves who betrayed their masters were rewarded. Sons informed on their fathers.

Cicero was among the victims. Antony had never forgiven him for the Philippics, the speeches attacking him after Caesar's death. Cicero was caught trying to flee Italy and was executed. His head and hands were brought to Antony and displayed in the Forum. Later sources, including Cassius Dio, report that Fulvia, Antony's wife, drove a pin through the severed tongue in mockery of his oratory, though this detail is likely an embellishment.

The confiscations were brutal but also effective. The triumvirs raised the forces they needed. The leading conspirators had already departed Rome. Brutus and Cassius moved east, raising forces in Macedonia and Asia Minor by levying heavy taxes and requisitions on the eastern provinces.

The conspirators had an army, but the assassination had already failed in every way that mattered. The conspirators had killed Caesar with no plan for what came next. They had not secured the loyalty of the legions. They had not controlled the public reaction. They had left Antony alive and free to act. They had dismissed Octavian as a sickly teenager with no political weight. Every one of those miscalculations would cost them. The Roman Republic they thought they were saving would not survive another decade. The men who killed Caesar in the name of liberty had set in motion the final destruction of everything they claimed to be defending.

Avenging Caesar

Mark Antony and Octavian led their armies eastward, proclaiming they would avenge Caesar's murder. They met the forces of the Liberators (those who had "liberated" Rome from tyranny) at Philippi in Macedonia in 42 BCE. Octavian was seriously ill during much of the campaign; as we noted before, his health had always been fragile. So, Antony took effective command of their forces.

The first engagement was tactically mixed. Antony defeated Cassius on one flank, while Brutus overran Octavian's position on the other. Cassius, unaware that Brutus had succeeded, received false reports of a general defeat and took his own life. It was a huge loss for the Liberators. Cassius was widely regarded as the more capable military commander of the two, and his death weakened their position considerably.

After weeks of maneuvering, the two sides met again. At the Second Battle of Philippi, the combined forces of Antony and Octavian defeated Brutus. His army collapsed, and Brutus committed suicide rather than be taken. The last serious military opposition to the Caesarian cause was finished.

A painting of the Battle of Philippi.[46]

The victory at Philippi settled who controlled the Roman world, but it did not settle who would dominate it. The division of territory that followed contained the seeds of a future conflict. Antony took the wealthy Eastern provinces—Egypt, Syria, and Asia Minor—where the tax revenues were enormous, and the resources of the Hellenistic world were within reach. Octavian was given Italy and the Western provinces—Gaul and Spain. On paper, this looked like an equal split. In practice, Antony had the richer share, and Octavian had the harder task. Italy was the political heart of Rome, but it was also where hundreds of thousands of veterans needed land. Settling them meant confiscating farms from existing owners, which caused bitterness and unrest. Antony could pursue glory in the East largely free of these pressures. Octavian had to manage a resentful Italy with limited funds and no military prestige to speak of.

The Second Triumvirate was renewed by the Treaty of Tarentum in 37 BCE, extending the arrangement for another five years, but the underlying competition for dominance was already pulling the two men apart. Antony emerged as the senior partner in the alliance after Philippi. As part of the political settlement, Octavian's sister, Octavia, married Antony, binding the alliance with a family tie.

Octavian's most pressing external threat was Sextus Pompey. The youngest son of Pompey the Great had seized Sicily and built a powerful fleet while the triumvirs were occupied with the Liberators. Sicily controlled the sea lanes that carried grain from Egypt and Africa to Rome. Sextus understood this. His fleet blockaded the Italian coast and intercepted grain shipments. By 39 BCE, his stranglehold had brought Italy close to famine. Grain shortages in Rome caused riots. The people's anger was directed toward Octavian, who was responsible for Italy and could not protect its food supply. The situation became so dangerous that the triumvirs were forced to negotiate. In the Pact of Misenum in 39 BCE, Octavian and Antony recognized Sextus's control of Sicily, Sardinia, Corsica, and the Peloponnese and promised him future political honors in exchange for his ending the blockade and allowing grain ships to pass. It was a humiliating concession, driven entirely by the threat of popular revolt in Rome.

The peace did not hold. Sextus and the triumvirs soon accused each other of violating the terms, and hostilities resumed. Octavian suffered serious naval setbacks in 38 BCE when his own attempts to dislodge Sextus failed badly. It was Agrippa, Octavian's most capable general, who solved the problem. He spent time building and training an entirely new fleet from scratch at Lake Avernus. At the naval Battle of Naulochus in 36 BCE, fought off the coast of Sicily, Agrippa destroyed Sextus's fleet. Sextus fled east and was later captured and killed. The defeat of Sextus transformed Octavian's position in the West. The grain supply was restored, the unrest in Rome ended, and his popularity recovered.

In the aftermath of Naulochus, Lepidus attempted to claim Sicily for himself, bringing his African legions and challenging Octavian's authority. Octavian outmaneuvered him politically—his soldiers defected rather than fight Caesar's heir—and stripped him of any real power. Lepidus had held the title of Pontifex Maximus since 44 BCE. Octavian allowed him to keep the title but exiled him from public life. He spent the remaining decades of his life under house arrest at Circeii. His removal was the end of the Second Triumvirate in any meaningful sense. The Roman world was now divided between two men.

The divide was not just territorial. It was becoming increasingly ideological. Antony spent more and more time in the East, drawn into the orbit of Cleopatra and the Hellenistic monarchies. He adopted Eastern dress and customs, distributed Roman territories to Cleopatra's children, and presented himself in ways that reflected the god Dionysus. Octavian watched all of this carefully and made sure Rome watched too. He positioned himself as the defender of Roman tradition, Italian values, and Republican custom. Propaganda began shaping the conflict before a single battle was fought. By the time the two men moved toward open war, Octavian had already won the battle in Rome.

Mark Antony and Cleopatra

After Philippi, Antony turned his attention to the East. He met Cleopatra at Tarsus in 41 BCE. Their alliance was as much political as personal. Antony needed Egypt's wealth and resources for his Eastern ambitions. Cleopatra needed Roman military power to secure her dynasty. The relationship served both of them.

In 40 BCE, Cleopatra gave birth to twins by Antony. A third child followed several years later.

Antony reorganized the Eastern provinces and launched a major invasion of Parthia in 36 BCE, partly to avenge Crassus and partly to rival the achievements of Alexander the Great. It failed badly. His army suffered serious losses, and he was forced into a costly retreat. The Parthian campaign damaged both his reputation and his military strength at a critical moment.

Meanwhile, Octavian was building his position in the West and conducting a propaganda campaign against his rival. In 32 BCE, he allegedly obtained Antony's will from the Vestal Virgins, whether legally or not, and read it aloud in the Senate. The will reportedly requested that Antony be buried in Alexandria alongside Cleopatra, suggesting he intended to shift the center of Roman power to Egypt. Octavian ensured this circulated widely. He framed the coming conflict not as another Roman civil war—the public had no appetite for more of those—but as a war between Rome and a foreign queen who had seduced a Roman commander away from his duties and his people. Cleopatra was portrayed as a dangerous Eastern temptress who had corrupted Antony and threatened to make Rome subservient to Egypt. Antony was not cast as a Roman rebel but as her instrument. It was skillful and deliberately constructed. Octavian understood that legitimacy mattered as much as an army did.

In 35 BCE, after the failure of his Parthian campaign, Octavia traveled to the East with money, troops, and supplies to support her husband. She reached Athens. Antony ordered her not to proceed further and refused to receive her. She returned to Rome.

In 34 BCE, Antony held the Donations of Alexandria, a public ceremony in which he and Cleopatra distributed territories across the East. Cleopatra was declared Queen of Kings, and her son Caesarion, by Caesar, was declared King of Kings. Her children with Antony received other Eastern territories. Some of these lands were Roman client kingdoms. The event was seen in Rome as Antony handing Roman possessions to a foreign queen and her children. It may have been intended partly as political theater to impress Eastern audiences, but in Rome, it played directly into Octavian's hands.

By 33 BCE, the Second Triumvirate had expired. Antony refused to relinquish his command. He had been designated consul for 31 BCE, but the escalating conflict made taking office impossible. Several of his allies and supporters defected as his position weakened. In 32 BCE, Antony formally divorced Octavia, Octavian's sister. By then, he was living openly with Cleopatra in Alexandria. The divorce gave Octavian a clear political advantage. Antony could now be portrayed not simply as a rival but as a Roman leader who had abandoned his Roman wife for a foreign queen.

That year, the Senate, acting under Octavian's influence, declared war on Cleopatra. Antony was stripped of his powers. Octavian had framed the conflict carefully. This was a war against a foreign queen, not a Roman civil war, and Antony was cast as her consort rather than as Rome's enemy.

Antony and Cleopatra assembled a large fleet and army in Greece, preparing for what appeared to be an invasion of Italy. Agrippa, Octavian's trusted general, moved first. He captured key ports along the Greek coast and strangled Antony's supply lines. Antony's forces began to suffer from the lack of food and from disease throughout the summer. His land army remained large on paper, but its fighting effectiveness declined.

In September 31 BCE, at Actium on the western coast of Greece, Antony attempted to break out of Octavian's naval blockade with his fleet. Agrippa outmaneuvered him. During the battle, Cleopatra withdrew with her squadron; whether this was a planned escape or a breakdown in coordination is debated by ancient sources and modern historians alike. Antony followed her. The bulk of his fleet was destroyed or surrendered. His land army, abandoned and leaderless, surrendered shortly afterward.

But Actium did not end the war immediately. Antony and Cleopatra still controlled Egypt, and Octavian spent the following year consolidating his victory before advancing on Alexandria.

Octavian marched on Egypt in 30 BCE. Antony's remaining forces melted away, and he eventually took his own life. Cleopatra, reportedly unwilling to be displayed in Octavian's triumph, did the same. Ancient sources describe her dying from a snakebite, though the exact circumstances are uncertain.

The conquest of Egypt was not simply a military victory. Octavian took the country as his personal domain rather than making it a standard Roman province. Its enormous agricultural wealth and the revenue flowing from its trade became his own private treasury. He banned senators from entering Egypt without his permission, ensuring that no rival could use its riches as a base for challenging him. The wealth of Egypt funded his armies, his building programs, and the political settlement that would follow. It was one of the foundations on which his dominance of Rome was built.

Caesarion, Cleopatra's son by Caesar and perhaps the only biological child of Julius Caesar, was executed after the conquest, almost certainly on Octavian's orders. He was a potential rival claimant to Caesar's legacy, after all. With Caesarion dead, no serious rival remained.

The Roman Republic was effectively dead. This was not simply the result of one man's ambition. The system had been failing for generations. The Senate had grown dependent on powerful individuals to manage a vast empire that its institutions were never designed to control. Armies had become loyal to their generals rather than to the state, a process that Caesar and those before him had accelerated. Extraordinary commands had been granted so routinely that they had become normal. After a century of political violence, assassination, and civil war, most Romans had stopped believing that the old order could deliver the stability they needed.

Octavian understood this. He preserved the forms of Republican government—the Senate, the magistracies, and the elections—while concentrating real power in his own hands. Within a few years, he would take the name Augustus and become Rome's first emperor, though he was careful never to call himself king. The Roman Republic had not been abolished. It had simply been made irrelevant.

Chapter 9: The Legacy of Julius Caesar

Caesar and the Death of the Roman Republic

Caesar was one of the most important figures in Western history. His campaigns, strategies, reforms, and writings left a mark on Rome and on Western civilization that can still be felt today. That legacy is complex and difficult to summarize.

When Caesar crossed the Rubicon, he triggered a civil war that engulfed the Mediterranean for years and dealt a severe blow to the Roman Republic, an institution already weakened by decades of internal conflict. He did not set out to destroy it. In the early stages of the conflict, his aim was more limited. He wanted to avoid prosecution by his enemies in the Senate and to retain the extraordinary powers he had earned through his campaigns. He believed this was his right. His victories made that position irreversible. By 45 BCE, he dominated the Roman world.

He made himself dictator, but he was not a conventional tyrant. He did not abolish Republican institutions. He worked through them and around them at the same time, accumulating powers and offices that stripped those institutions of any real independence. He limited the independence of the two consuls, reducing them from chief magistrates of the state to men who functioned within the system he created. He expanded and packed the Senate, weakening the influence of the old aristocratic families and ensuring that the Senate could not act against him. He limited the independence of the tribunes—the traditional champions of the Roman people—though he did not formally abolish the office. He named Octavian as his heir in his will, but he did not create a legal mechanism for hereditary rule. The question of how power would pass after his death was left unresolved.

Still, the damage to the Republican system was nonetheless real and lasting. After his assassination, the old order could not be restored. The conspirators may have wanted that to happen, but the institutions were no longer in place to allow that to happen smoothly.

It should be acknowledged that the Roman Republic was already in serious difficulty before Caesar even crossed the Rubicon. For almost a century, ever since the time of the Gracchi brothers, the state had been shaken by political violence, the rise of military strongmen, and the breakdown of the old order among the senatorial elite. Whether the Roman Republic would have survived without Caesar is a question that cannot be answered with confidence. Some historians argue it was already doomed. Others point out that the idea of the republic remained powerful and that large parts of the Roman elite remained genuinely committed to it. It is possible, though of course not certain, that a victory for the Pompeian cause might have allowed some version of the old government to continue, as Sulla had briefly done after his own civil war. Caesar's victory made that question moot. Too many of the old Republican elite had died. Those who replaced them were willing to work with an autocrat. His victories sealed the transformation, and his system of government, however improvised, paved the way for the imperial order that followed.

Julius Caesar and the Rise of Europe

Caesar is often ranked among the greatest commanders in history, alongside Alexander the Great and Genghis Khan. His campaigns extended Roman power into regions that would shape the future of an entire continent. Military academies have studied his tactics and strategies for centuries. Napoleon was one of his most enthusiastic students.

The conquest of Gaul was his most important military achievement. Before it, Rome had been primarily a Mediterranean power. After the defeat of Vercingetorix at Alesia, it became a continental one. The Roman occupation of Gaul—what is now France, Belgium, and parts of Switzerland—unified a fragmented region under a common administrative and cultural system. The Latin language, Roman law, urban infrastructure, and eventually Christianity spread through these territories in the centuries that followed. What long-term shape Gaul might have taken without

Roman conquest is impossible to say, but it is fair to say that the foundations of what became French civilization were built on Roman ones.

Caesar also conducted expeditions beyond the Rhine into Germanic territory, crossing the river and displaying Roman power to the tribes on the other side. These were raids rather than conquests. There was no permanent annexation, but Roman contact with the Germanic world had consequences. The cultural exchange between Rome and the Germanic peoples who eventually succeeded Roman power in the West influenced the kingdoms that emerged after Rome's fall. Charlemagne's Frankish empire and the Holy Roman Empire that developed from it drew extensively on Roman models, institutions, and symbols.

Caesar's raids in Britain in 55 and 54 BCE produced no permanent occupation, but they showed that the island could be invaded and that it was worth the effort. Nearly a century later, Emperor Claudius ordered the conquest of Britain in 43 CE. The resulting province of Britannia was Roman for nearly four centuries and left lasting imprints on the island's language, religion, urban geography, and legal traditions. These are long chains of consequence, so it would be an overstatement to lay all of them at Caesar's feet. But his campaigns set many of them in motion.

Julius Caesar and Architecture

Caesar left a visible mark on Rome itself. He built on a large scale, partly to enhance the city's grandeur, partly to stimulate the economy, and partly to associate himself with monuments that would outlast him. His most significant contribution was the Forum Iulium (the Forum of Caesar), which set a new model for civic architecture and inspired the later forums of Augustus and his successors. The Basilica Julia, which he commissioned on the southern edge of the Roman Forum, was a large multi-aisled structure with interior colonnades that became the center of legal and commercial activity in the city. The Temple of Venus Genetrix, which stood at the far end of his Forum, tied divine ancestry to a permanent religious monument at the heart of Rome.

The architectural styles and techniques developed under Caesar and Augustus became the classical template, replicated by Romanized elites across the empire. They later inspired architects from the Renaissance to the modern era. Many of the public buildings, courthouses, and civic institutions of later European and American cities were built in direct imitation of Roman models.

Caesar's Calendar

The calendar Caesar introduced in 45 BCE was one of his most lasting achievements. The reform was the work of Egyptian astronomers working at his direction, notably Sosigenes of Alexandria. It replaced the old Roman calendar, which had drifted badly out of alignment with the solar year, with a system of 365 days and a leap year every 4 years. The new calendar kept Rome's traditional festivals and religious dates in place, which made it easier for people to accept. It was adopted across the empire and remained in use throughout the Western world long after Rome had fallen.

By the late 16th century, the Julian calendar had drifted roughly ten days out of alignment with the solar year, prompting Pope Gregory XIII to commission a reform. The Gregorian calendar, introduced in 1582, removed ten accumulated days and refined the leap-year rule for century years. Britain did not adopt the Gregorian calendar until 1752. Some Orthodox churches continue to use the Julian calendar to this day. The month of July still retains Caesar's name in most major European languages.

Propaganda

Caesar understood that political power required narrative as well as force. His *Commentarii* on the Gallic Wars and on the civil war are classics of Latin prose and remain among the most readable accounts of ancient warfare. They are also works of propaganda. They are written in the third person, presenting Caesar as a figure of cool rationality and consistent success. Mistakes are minimized or reframed as the failures of subordinates or the unreliability of allies. Modern historians treat the *Commentarii* as valuable historical sources while acknowledging their selective and self-serving character. These were not simply private memoirs but public communications. Caesar had them circulated in Rome while he was still on campaign, keeping the Roman public informed—and impressed—with regular accounts of his successes in Gaul. It was a deliberate use of propaganda that had not really been seen before in the Roman world.

His building program served similar purposes. The Temple of Venus Genetrix reinforced his family's claimed divine descent. The Forum Iulium created a monument in his name at the center of Rome. His mercy toward defeated enemies was itself a form of propaganda, as it was intended to show that his dominance was benevolent rather than tyrannical.

The propaganda methods Caesar developed were absorbed and refined by Augustus, becoming the standard toolkit of Roman imperial ideology. Later European rulers, from medieval kings to early modern monarchs, drew on the same traditions. The idea that a strong ruler legitimizes his power through victory, public works, divine favor, and the language of restoration rather than innovation is, in many ways, a Caesarian inheritance.

The Principate

Caesar's assassination might have ended his political legacy entirely had he not made one crucial decision: naming Octavian as his heir. Octavian lacked Caesar's military genius but proved his equal in political intelligence and considerably his superior in patience and caution. He learned from Caesar's example and perhaps even more from Caesar's mistakes. Caesar had taken power openly and provoked the elite until they killed him. Augustus accumulated the same power gradually, within Republican forms, and died in his bed after forty years of serving as emperor.

The system Augustus built rested on foundations Caesar had laid. The weakening of the Senate's independence, the subordination of the consulship, the control of military patronage, and the use of divine ancestry for political legitimacy were all precedents set by Caesar. Augustus extended citizenship to provincial elites selectively—broad universal citizenship came only in 212 CE under Caracalla—but the process Caesar began of incorporating provincial communities into the Roman political structure continued under his heir and successors. Augustus developed what became the imperial cult, the veneration of the emperor as a divine or semi-divine figure, though in Rome itself, he was careful to present himself as First Citizen rather than a god. He reserved the more explicit divine honors for the Eastern provinces, where such traditions were already established. Official deification came after death, not during life. The ideological claim that a single strong ruler was necessary to protect the people, unify the state, and maintain Rome's greatness was a Caesarian inheritance, developed by Augustus and passed to the emperors who followed.

That system endured in the West until 476 CE and in the East, in the form of the Byzantine Empire, until 1453. Whether it would have developed as it did without Caesar is impossible to say with any certainty. What can be said is that his victories, his methods, his institutions, and his heir shaped the structure of the Roman Empire, and the Roman Empire shaped the world that surrounded it.

Bust of Augustus[47]

The Contested Legacy of Caesar

Caesar was one of the most important figures in the history of the Western world. People who change the course of history tend to be controversial, and Caesar is no exception. His contemporaries were divided on his legacy almost immediately after his death. Cicero condemned him as an enemy of freedom. His supporters revered him as a man who had brought glory, order, and justice to Rome. Augustus carefully cultivated his adopted father's memory and referred to him publicly as his father throughout his reign.

In 42 BCE, the Senate officially deified Caesar, an act that made him Divus Julius (the Divine Julius). He was the first Roman to be formally deified by the state. The timing was politically useful to Augustus, who became the son of a god. Ancient sources report that a comet appeared in the sky during the funeral games held in Caesar's honor shortly after his death. It is known as the Sidus Iulium, or Julian star. Augustus seized on this as evidence of Caesar's divinity and had the comet incorporated into portraits and monuments. A temple to Divus Julius was built in the Roman Forum, on the spot where Caesar's body had been cremated. The cult of the deified Caesar became one of the foundations of the imperial religion that developed under Augustus, and the pattern—a deceased emperor declared divine and his successor ruling as the son of a god—became the template for imperial succession.

Emperors adopted the name Caesar to associate themselves with his legacy. The title passed from ruler to successor across Europe and beyond. In the Germanic world, it became kaiser. In the Slavic world, it became tsar (or czar). Both are direct corruptions of Caesar, used by rulers claiming the legitimacy of the Roman imperial tradition. The word outlived the empire that produced it by more than a millennium. It became synonymous with supreme authority in a way that transcended any specific political system. It was a symbol of power so potent that rulers who had no ethnic or territorial connection to Rome still reached for it.

Russian rulers developed the ideology of Moscow as the Third Rome, claiming inheritance from the Roman imperial system. After the fall of Constantinople in 1453, the Ottoman sultans also claimed to be heirs to the Roman imperial tradition. In Byzantium, the title kaisar evolved into a senior court rank rather than the main imperial title, which became basileus, but it remained in use until the empire's end.

The term Caesarism entered the political vocabulary in the 19th century to describe the rule of one man through military prestige and popular authority, bypassing or subordinating traditional institutions. The French political theorist Auguste Romieu used it in the 1850s to describe Napoleon III's regime, and Napoleon III himself explicitly invoked Caesar as a model and predecessor, commissioning a biography of him and presenting his own rule as a modern version of Caesar's. The idea was that Caesar—and by extension Napoleon—had not destroyed the legitimate government but had rescued a society whose existing institutions could no longer govern. The 19th-century historian Theodor Mommsen made a version of this argument in his influential history of Rome, portraying Caesar as a great man who recognized that the Roman Republic was finished and acted accordingly. Max Weber later used Caesar as a reference point for his concept of charismatic authority, the idea that certain leaders derive their legitimacy not from tradition or law but from the force of their own personality and the belief of their followers. Whether or not one accepts these ideas, they show that Caesar became something more than a historical figure. He became a political archetype and a name associated with a recurring problem in how societies manage the tension between strong leadership and institutional constraints.

The assessment of Caesar has never been settled because it cannot be. Different eras have found different things in him. To Cicero and the Republicans of his own time, he was a tyrant who destroyed the liberty of the Roman aristocracy. To his own soldiers and the urban poor of Rome, he was a patron, a protector, and a source of glory. To Augustus and the imperial tradition, he was the divine originator of a system that brought peace after a century of chaos. To medieval rulers, he was one example among several of legitimate imperial authority. To Renaissance humanists, he exemplified what Machiavelli called *virtù*—the capacity of an exceptional individual to impose his will on circumstance. To Enlightenment republicans and French revolutionaries, he was the destroyer of the Roman Republic and a warning about the danger of military populism. To 19th-century nationalists and imperialists, he was proof that great men make history. To fascist movements of the 20th century, he was a symbol of strong leadership, national renewal, and contempt for parliamentary weakness. To modern historians attentive to the human cost of conquest, he is the man responsible for the deaths and enslavement of a large number of people in Gaul in a campaign whose scale and methods have led some scholars to apply the word genocide, however contested that term is when applied to the ancient world.

Modern historians debate Caesar without reaching any consensus. Was he a revolutionary or essentially conservative? Was he a man who wanted to preserve Rome's power and his own position within it rather than transform its social order? Did he genuinely seek to create a monarchy, or was he accumulating power pragmatically without a fixed goal in mind? Was the Roman Republic already collapsing before he crossed the Rubicon, making his role more of a catalyst than a cause? Was he primarily a reformer who saw clearly what Rome needed or an opportunist who used the language of reform to justify his personal ambition? The ancient sources do not resolve these questions, and neither do the modern ones.

What can be said is that the Caesar later ages remembered often reflect the preoccupations of those ages as much as the man himself. The Caesar of the Renaissance is not quite the same figure as the Caesar of the Enlightenment or the Caesar of the 19th century or the Caesar of today. Each generation has reconstructed him in light of its own anxieties about power, liberty, greatness, and violence. That is the fate of figures who genuinely change the world. They become screens onto which later eras project their own questions. Caesar has been a tyrant, a founder, a strategist, a demagogue, a reformer, and a warning. He will probably continue to be all of these things because the questions his life raises—about how power is seized and justified, about what individuals can do to history and what history does to individuals, and about the price of greatness—are not questions that will ever go away.

Conclusion

Caesar's life does not give us any easy conclusions. It never has. He was a priest and a politician before he was a general. He was a reformer and a destroyer at the same time. He used the Republican system to climb to the top and then dismantled the checks that the system depended on. He was capable of extraordinary mercy and extraordinary ruthlessness, sometimes within the same campaign.

This book has traced his career from its beginnings to its consequences. The wars in Gaul and the chaos of the late Roman Republic. The crossing of the Rubicon and the civil wars that followed. The brief dictatorship and the assassination on the Ides of March. The long aftermath—the second round of civil wars, the rise of Augustus, and the transformation of Rome into an empire that endured for centuries in the West and over a millennium in the East.

Along the way, this book has tried to show the man behind the legend. His relationship with Cleopatra, which was as political as it was personal. His genius for warfare and the principles that made him one of the most studied commanders in history. His instinct for propaganda and the ways he shaped his own image. The calendar that still structures our year. The buildings that changed Rome's skyline. The writings that are still read two thousand years after his death.

There are many myths surrounding Caesar, and they are largely his own creation. He wrote his own history, literally. This book has tried to separate what is known from what is claimed and to note where the evidence runs out and interpretation begins.

What emerges is a figure who resists a simple verdict. He was not simply a tyrant, and he was not simply a savior. He was a man of his time who pushed his things past their breaking point. Yes, the Roman Republic was already under enormous strain before Caesar crossed the Rubicon. Whether it would have survived without him is impossible to know. What is known is that it did not survive and that the system Augustus built on the ruins of it shaped the political world of Europe, the Middle East, and beyond for more than a thousand years.

Caesar's name became a title. His methods became a template. His story became a mirror in which later ages saw their own questions about power, liberty, and the cost of greatness reflected back at them.

That is still true today. The tension Caesar embodied, between the needs of a state and the ambitions of individuals, between institutions and the men who claim to serve them, and between order and freedom, has not been resolved. It probably cannot be. Understanding how Rome navigated that tension, and ultimately failed to, is not merely an exercise in ancient history. It is a way of thinking about how power works, how republics weaken, and what is at stake when they do.

If you enjoyed this book, a review on Amazon would be greatly appreciated because it would mean a lot to hear from you.

To leave a review:

1. Open your camera app.
2. Point your mobile device at the QR code.
3. The review page will appear in your web browser.

Thanks for your support!

Here's another book by Enthralling History that you might like

Free limited time bonus

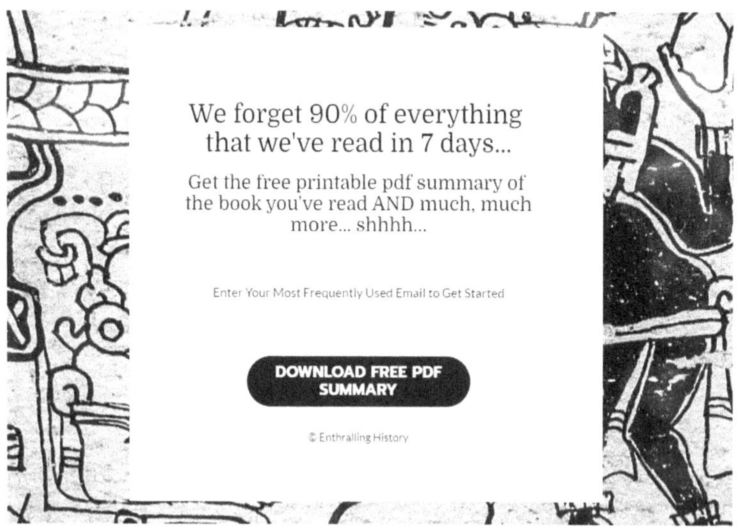

Stop for a moment. We have a free bonus set up for you. The problem is this: we forget 90% of everything that we read after 7 days. Crazy fact, right? Here's the solution: we've created a printable, 1-page pdf summary for this book that you're reading now. All you have to do to get your free pdf summary is to go to the following website:
https://livetolearn.lpages.co/enthrallinghistory/

Or, Scan the QR code!

Once you do, it will be intuitive. Enjoy, and thank you!

Bibliography

Part 1: Roman Military History

Appian, *The Histories,* Loeb Classical Library, 1913.

Dionysius of Halicarnassus, *Roman Antiquities,* Loeb Classical Library, 1940.

Goldsworthy, Adrien, *Roman Warfare,* Wellington House, 2000.

Group of Authors, *Historical Evolution of Roman Infantry, Arms and Armour,* Worcester Polytechnic Institute, 2018.

Harkness, Albert, *The Military System of the Romans,* University of New York, 1887.

Josephus, Flavius, *Wars of the Jews,*

Julius Caesar, *Commentarii De Bello Gallico,* W. J. Gage & Co., 1890.

M. Carry & H. H. Scullard, *A History of Rome down to the Reign of Constantine,* The Macmillan Press Ltd., 1975.

Mashkin, Nikolai, *A History of Ancient Rome,* Gospolitizdat, 1956.

Mesihović, Salmedin, *Orbis Romanvs,* University of Sarajevo, 2015.

Mirković, Miroslava, *Istorija Rimske države,* Službeni glasnik, 2014.

Octavianus Augustus, *Res Gestae divi Augusti,*

Petković, Žarko*, Pad rimske republike,* Filip Višnjić, 2018.

Polybius, *Histories,* Matica Srpska, 1988.

Rostovtzeff, Michael, *A History of the Ancient World: Volume II, Rome,* Oxford University, 1933.

Sallust, *The Jugurthine War and the Conspiracy of Catiline,* Roman Roads Media, 2015.

Titus Livius, *From the Founding of the City,* 2012.

Vegetius, *De re Militari*, University of Nottingham, 1962.

Zosimus, *New History*, 2017.

Part 2: Julius Caesar

Arena, Valentina. *Libertas and the Practice of Politics in the Late Roman Republic*. Cambridge: Cambridge University Press, 2012.

Billows, Richard A. *Julius Caesar: The Colossus of Rome*. New York: Routledge, 2008.

Bradford, Ernle. *Julius Caesar: The Pursuit of Power*. New York: Open Road Media, 2014.

Caesar, Julius. *Commentaries*. London: Penguin, 1985.

Chrissanthos, Stefan G. *The Year of Julius and Caesar: 59 BC and the Transformation of the Roman Republic*. Baltimore: Johns Hopkins University Press, 2019.

Cicero. *Selected Writings*. London: Penguin, 2001.

Goldsworthy, Adrian. *Augustus: From Revolutionary to Emperor*. London: Weidenfeld & Nicolson, 2014.

Goldsworthy, Adrian. *Caesar*. London: Weidenfeld & Nicolson, 2013.

Goldsworthy, Adrian. *Caesar's Civil War: 49–44 BC*. New York: Routledge, 2013.

Holmes, T. Rice. *Ancient Britain and the Invasions of Julius Caesar*. DigiCat, 2022.

Krebs, Christopher. "More Than Words: The *Commentarii* in Their Propagandistic Context." In *The Cambridge Companion to the Writings of Julius Caesar*, 29–42. Cambridge: Cambridge University Press, 2018.

Montemurro, Nicholas, Alberto Benet, and Michael T. Lawton. "Julius Caesar's Epilepsy: Was It Caused by a Brain Arteriovenous Malformation?" *World Neurosurgery* 84, no. 6 (2015): 1985–1987.

Morrell, Kit. *Pompey, Cato, and the Governance of the Roman Empire*. Oxford: Oxford University Press, 2017.

Morstein-Marx, Robert. *Julius Caesar and the Roman People*. Cambridge: Cambridge University Press, 2021.

Plutarch. *Lives of the Noble Grecians and Romans*. London: Penguin, 1987.

Rosenstein, Nathan, and Robert Morstein-Marx, eds. *A Companion to the Roman Republic*. Malden, MA: Wiley-Blackwell, 2011.

Taylor, Philip M. *Munitions of the Mind: A History of Propaganda from the Ancient World to the Present Era*. Manchester: Manchester University Press, 2013.

Image Sources

1 https://commons.wikimedia.org/wiki/File:The_Intervention_of_the_Sabine_Women_-_David_(Louvre_INV_3691).jpg

2 https://commons.wikimedia.org/wiki/File:Furius-Camillus.jpg

3 . National Gallery of Art, CC0, via Wikimedia Commons, https://commons.wikimedia.org/wiki/File:Pseudo_Melioli,_Romans_Passing_Under_the_Yoke,_late_15th_-_early_16th_century,_NGA_43922.jpg

4 . Marie-Lan Nguyen / Wikimedia Commons, https://commons.wikimedia.org/wiki/File:Pyrrhus_MAN_Napoli_Inv6150_n03.jpg

5 . Piom, translation by Pamela Butler, CC BY-SA 3.0 <http://creativecommons.org/licenses/by-sa/3.0/>, via Wikimedia Commons, https://commons.wikimedia.org/wiki/File:Pyrrhic_War_Italy_en.svg

6 . This image has been created during "DensityDesign Integrated Course Final Synthesis Studio" at Politecnico di Milano, organized by DensityDesign Research Lab in 2016. Credits goes to Agata Brilli, CC BY-SA 4.0 <https://creativecommons.org/licenses/by-sa/4.0>, via Wikimedia Commons, https://commons.wikimedia.org/wiki/File:Domain_changes_during_the_Punic_Wars.gif

7 https://commons.wikimedia.org/wiki/File:Corvus_%C3%A4nterbrygga.png

8 . This image has been created during "DensityDesign Integrated Course Final Synthesis Studio" at Politecnico di Milano, organized by DensityDesign Research Lab in 2016. Credits goes to Agata Brilli, CC BY-SA 4.0 <https://creativecommons.org/licenses/by-sa/4.0>, via Wikimedia Commons, https://commons.wikimedia.org/wiki/File:Domain_changes_during_the_Punic_Wars.gif

9 https://commons.wikimedia.org/wiki/File:Mommsen_p265.jpg

10 https://commons.wikimedia.org/wiki/File:Scipio_at_the_deathbed_of_Masinissa_(C20).jpg

11 .This image has been created during "DensityDesign Integrated Course Final Synthesis Studio" at Politecnico di Milano, organized by DensityDesign Research Lab in 2016. Credits goes to Agata Brilli, CC BY-SA 4.0 <https://creativecommons.org/licenses/by-sa/4.0>, via Wikimedia Commons https://commons.wikimedia.org/wiki/File:Domain_changes_during_the_Punic_Wars.gif

12 .José Luiz Bernardes Ribeiro. This file is licensed under the Creative Commons Attribution-Share Alike 4.0 International license, https://commons.wikimedia.org/wiki/File:Bust_of_Marius_(GL_319)_-_Glyptothek_-_Munich_-_Germany_2017.jpg

13 https://commons.wikimedia.org/wiki/File:Jugurtha_captured.jpg

14 .No machine-readable author provided. MatthiasKabel assumed (based on copyright claims)., CC BY-SA 3.0 <http://creativecommons.org/licenses/by-sa/3.0/>, via Wikimedia Commons, https://commons.wikimedia.org /wiki/File:Roman_aquila.jpg

15 https://commons.wikimedia.org/wiki/File:Retrato_de_Julio_C%C3%A9sar _(26724093101)_(cropped).jpg

16 https://commons.wikimedia.org/wiki/File:A_Chronicle_of_England_-_Page_005_-_The_Standard_Bearer_of_the_Tenth_Legion.jpg

17 https://commons.wikimedia.org/wiki/File:Siege-alesia-vercingetorix-jules-cesar.jpg

18 .Vatican Museums, CC BY-SA 4.0 <https://creativecommons.org/licenses/by-sa/4.0>, via Wikimedia Commons, https://commons.wikimedia.org/wiki /File:Augustus_of_Prima_Porta_(inv._2290).jpg

19 .ColdEel, CC BY-SA 3.0 <https://creativecommons.org/licenses/by-sa/3.0>, via Wikimedia Commons, https://commons.wikimedia.org/wiki/File:Roman-Empire-43BC.png

20 .Cristiano64, CC BY-SA 3.0 <http://creativecommons.org/licenses/by-sa/3.0/>, via Wikimedia Commons, https://commons.wikimedia.org/wiki/File: Impero_romano_sotto_Ottaviano_Augusto_30aC_-_6dC.jpg

21 https://commons.wikimedia.org/wiki/File:Otto_Albert_Koch_Varusschlacht_1909.jpg

22 .CristianChirita, CC BY-SA 3.0 <http://creativecommons.org/licenses/by-sa/3.0/>, via Wikimedia Commons, https://commons.wikimedia.org/wiki/ File:Engineering_corps_traian_s_column_river_crossing.jpg

23 .NumisAntica, CC BY-SA 3.0 NL <https://creativecommons.org/licenses/by-sa/3.0/nl/deed.en>, via Wikimedia Commons, https://commons.wikimedia.org/wiki/File:Romeinse_keizers_Gordianus_III_antoninianus_Antiochie_243-244.jpg

24 .FropFrop, CC BY-SA 4.0 <https://creativecommons.org/licenses/by-sa/4.0>, via Wikimedia Commons, https://commons.wikimedia.org/wiki/File: Lorica_segmentata_remains_and_recreation.jpg

25 https://commons.wikimedia.org/wiki/File:5_Aurei,_Diocletian_and_ Maximianus_Herculius,_Elephantenquadriga,_Rome,_287_AD_-_Bode-Museum_-_DSC02724.JPG

26 https://commons.wikimedia.org/wiki/File:Battle_of_Adrianople_378_en.svg

27 https://commons.wikimedia.org/wiki/File:Visigoths_sack_Rome.jpg

28 Portasa Cristian, CC0, via Wikimedia Commons https://commons. wikimedia.org/wiki/File:Roman_Republic_and_its_cities_in_100_BC.png

29 https://commons.wikimedia.org/wiki/File;Julius_Caesar_Italian_marble_19th_c..jpg

30 https://commons.wikimedia.org/wiki/File:Sulla_Glyptothek_Munich_309.jpg

31 Mary Harrsch, CC BY-SA 4.0 <https://creativecommons.org/licenses/by-sa/4.0>, via Wikimedia Commons, https://commons.wikimedia.org/wiki/File:The_First_ Triumvirate_of_the_Roman_Republic_720X480.jpg

32 Glauco92, CC BY-SA 3.0 <https://creativecommons.org/licenses/by-sa/3.0>, via Wikimedia Commons, https://commons.wikimedia.org/wiki/File:Cicero_-_Musei_Capitolini.JPG

33 William Robert Shepherd, CC BY-SA 4.0 <https://creativecommons.org/licenses/by-sa/4.0>, via Wikimedia Commons; https://commons.wikimedia.org/wiki/File:Gaul_in_the_Time_of_Caesar.jpg

34 https://commons.wikimedia.org/wiki/File:Il_ponte_di_Cesare_sul_Reno.jpg

35 https://commons.wikimedia.org/wiki/File:Lionel_Royer_-_Vercingetorix_Throwing_down_His_Weapons_at_the_feet_of_Julius_Caesar.jpg

36 Prioryman, CC BY-SA 3.0 <https://creativecommons.org/licenses/by-sa/3.0>, via Wikimedia Commons; https://commons.wikimedia.org/wiki/File: Cato_Volubilis_bronze_bust.jpg

37 https://commons.wikimedia.org/wiki/File:Battle_of_Pharsalus,_48_BC.png

38 https://commons.wikimedia.org/wiki/File:Kleopatra-VII.-Altes-Museum-Berlin1.jpg

39 https://commons.wikimedia.org/wiki/File:Battle_of_the_Nile_(M._Merian).png

40 George E. Koronaios, CC BY-SA 4.0 <https://creativecommons.org/licenses/by-sa/4.0>, via Wikimedia Commons, https://commons.wikimedia.org/wiki/File: Portrait_of_Julius_Caesar_(1st_cent._B.C.)_at_the_Archaeological_Museum_of_Sparta_on_15_May_2019.jpg

41 Sdwelch1031, CC0, via Wikimedia Commons. https://commons.wikimedia.org/wiki/File:Caesarion.jpg

42 [1], CC BY-SA 4.0 <https://creativecommons.org/licenses/by-sa/4.0>, via Wikimedia Commons;

https://commons.wikimedia.org/wiki/File:Battle_of_Munda,_45_BC_(Initial_deployment_of_troops).jpg

43 Ashmolean Museum of Art and Archaeology, CC BY 2.0 <https://creativecommons.org/licenses/by/2.0>, via Wikimedia Commons, https://commons.wikimedia.org/wiki/File:Roman_coin,_denarius_of_Julius_Caeser_(FindID_800905).jpg

44 José Luiz Bernardes Ribeiro; https://commons.wikimedia.org/wiki/File:Forum_of_Julius_Caesar_and_Temple_of_Venus_Genitrix_-_Roman_Forums_-_Rome_2016.jpg

45 https://commons.wikimedia.org/wiki/File:Assassination_of_Julius_Caesar_for_Historia_de_Europa.jpg

46 https://commons.wikimedia.org/wiki/File:Pauwels_Casteels_-_The_Death_of_Brutus_and_Cassius_at_the_Battle_of_Philippi.jpg

47 Dan Mihai Pitea, CC BY-SA 4.0 <https://creativecommons.org/licenses/by-sa/4.0>, via Wikimedia Commons; https://commons.wikimedia.org/wiki/File:Glyptothek_M%C3%BCnchen_%E2%80%93_18.04.2022_%E2%80%93_Augustus_Bevilacqua_(4).jpg

www.ingramcontent.com/pod-product-compliance
Lightning Source LLC
LaVergne TN
LVHW010615100826
845148LV00014B/2978

9798887657035